EXIT EMPEROR
KIM JONG-IL

NOTES FROM HIS FORMER MENTOR

ALSO BY JOHN CHA

Kim Jong Il and Cinema Politica, translation

Willow Tree Shade: The Susan Ahn Cuddy Story

The Do or Die Entrepreneur

ALSO BY K.J. SOHN

Kim Jong-il Report

Documentary Kim Jong-il

EXIT EMPEROR
KIM JONG-IL

NOTES FROM HIS FORMER MENTOR

John H. Cha, with K. J. Sohn

abbott press®

A DIVISION OF WRITER'S DIGEST

EXIT EMPEROR KIM JONG-IL

Abbott Press books may be ordered through booksellers or by contacting:

Abbott Press
1663 Liberty Drive
Bloomington, IN 47403
www.abbottpress.com
Phone: 1-866-697-5310

ISBN: 978-1-4582-0216-1 (sc)
ISBN: 978-1-4582-0218-5 (hc)
ISBN: 978-1-4582-0217-8 (e)

Library of Congress Control Number: 2012903330

Printed in the United States of America

Abbott Press rev. date: 02/27/2012

For the people of North Korea

CONTENTS

PREFACE

I have the dubious honor of having lived under North Korean rule for three months in 1950 during the Korean War. I was four years and seven months old at the time, and the North Korean soldiers—then occupiers of Seoul—taught me a song praising "the Great General Kim Il-sung." I used to run around and sing it all the time, much to my mother's consternation. When she tried to get me to stop it, I would sing louder and longer, obstinate and persistent, especially when she scolded me for my performance. Apparently, it was a catchy tune. I don't remember the words or the melody to the song now.

Sometimes I wonder how my life would have turned out had the North Korean forces succeeded in overtaking the southern half of the peninsula. There would be just one Korea now, not two, and I would most likely still be singing Kim Il-sung's praises today, even sixteen years after his death. This leads to the debated and controversial question of whether Kim Il-sung was truly a great leader. Twenty-three million North Koreans seem to believe that he was, and if just numbers count, 23 million people cannot be wrong. But I suspect that the North Korean people have been bamboozled over the years. As great as Kim Il-sung is believed to be in the minds of the North Korean people, they have not been told everything. In my interviews with former residents of North Korea, I am continually surprised how little they know about the Kim family or world affairs. When one man rules a nation of people for forty-six years, there is bound to be corruption of power, as Lord Acton (1834-1902), British historian and moralist, said, "Power tends to corrupt, and absolute power corrupts absolutely. Great men are almost always bad men."

Lord Acton was referring to the myriad despotic kings, rulers, conquerors, and corrupt popes who had preceded him. He wasn't referring to Kim Il-sung, who emerged ten years after Acton's death, but he does seem to fit Acton's profile. Born in 1912, Kim Il-sung took control of North Korea in 1948 and held power until he died in 1994. This means that, according to Lord Acton's premise, Kim Il-sung had more than enough opportunity to become corrupt. Moreover, he passed his power on to his son, Kim Jong-il, who in turn has selected his third son, Kim Jong-un, to succeed him. They are transferring power as if they were passing on a family emblem from one generation to the next. There is something seedy and unholy about this practice, especially when you consider how much less than spectacular the first two Kims have performed in terms of ensuring any quality of life for the North Korean people.

Enter Hwang Jang-yop, a man who witnessed the Kim family's corruption of power firsthand. As a young man full of ideals, Hwang was swept up by the fervor to build a utopia in North Korea. He went on to become a member of the elite circle of power as the general secretariat of the Workers' Party of North Korea, until he defected to South Korea in 1997.

Born in 1923, Hwang Jang-yop attended Pyongyang Commerce School. Upon graduating, he went to Japan and studied law. In 1946, he joined the Workers' Party, taking his first step toward becoming a part of the ruling class of North Korea. He studied philosophy at Moscow University from 1949 to 1953, and upon his return, taught philosophy at Kim Il-sung University. He became the president of Kim Il-sung University in 1965, and then, in 1972, the chairman of the Supreme People's Assembly.

Of all his accomplishments in North Korea, he is most noted for being the architect of the *JuChe* (literally translated as "self-reliance") philosophy, which defines the guiding principles for North Korean society as a whole. By design, *JuChe* was a utopian endeavor, a map for building an ideal society; but his lifetime work was bastardized into an instrument for what he feared the most, a totalitarian dictatorship.

I met Hwang Jang-yop for the first time in Seoul in the fall of 2003. K.J. Sohn, my co-author and former research fellow at the National Intelligence Service (NIS) of Korea, took me to Hwang's office, where I was first greeted by several NIS agents. They asked me to hold my arms out and then patted me down. Sohn had forewarned me about the security check required by the NIS, so I went along with the process. One of the agents asked me for identification, and I gave him my passport, which he photocopied. Another agent asked me about my occupation and the purpose of my visit. I replied that I was there to give Mr. Hwang copies of my books and conduct an interview. He took some notes and let me go inside.

Sohn and I sat down in the reception area, and shortly afterward, Hwang walked in from an adjoining room. Wearing a plain suit and a tie, he stood about five feet seven. I stood up and shook his hand, bowing at the same time. There was a certain aura about him and a genuine, dignified manner. It is not often that I feel so drawn to a person whom I meet for the first time, but I felt a charismatic energy emanating from him. His eyes were steady and unassuming—a bit sad perhaps—yet he made me feel welcome without saying a word. The initial silence that usually comes with a first meeting didn't feel awkward at all. It helped to have a mutual acquaintance by the name of Young Paik, a gentleman I had written about in a book entitled *The Do or Die Entrepreneur: A Korean American Businessman's Journey.* Young Paik was involved in facilitating Mr. Hwang's defection from North Korea in 1997, and Hwang regarded Paik as his younger brother.

"How is Mr. Young Paik?" he asked.

"He is fine. He sends you his regards," I replied.

He smiled and said, "He escaped in 1951. I left forty-six years later. We are fellow defectors."

Sohn and I smiled and nodded. I asked, "How is your health?"

He replied with a sigh, "My health is excellent. But I feel stifled. I can't go anywhere freely on my own. It's like I'm locked up in a prison." He finished and glanced at the agent who was seated by the door. I followed Hwang's eyes to the agent, who didn't show any reaction to Hwang's plaintive remark that was directed toward the agency. The agent was just doing his job, and he didn't appear too interested in our conversation. He was one of many South Korean agents who were there to protect Hwang from possible attacks by North Korean agents. Kim Jong-il had publicly called for Hwang's assassination when he defected to the South Korean Embassy in Beijing.

Hwang's defection was widely reported in the press, especially in East Asia. Headline after headline heralded the story of Hwang, the highest-ranking official to defect North Korea to date, an elite among the elite. The international community was abuzz over his actions.

What I was most curious about—along with millions of people in Korea and abroad—was his motivation for turning his back on the ruling elite that he had served for so many decades. His decision to defect must not have been an easy one. By defecting, he knew that he was putting his family, friends, and colleagues in jeopardy. Yet he had carried out the unthinkable because he believed it was the right thing to do. I wanted to know what led him to his decision.

Understanding Hwang, however, required considerable effort on my part. First, I had to read all the books he had written in order to come up with any sort of intelligent questions for him. His frequent references to dialectic materialism, Marxism, and Stalinism also added more volumes of books to my reading list. Thanks to Sohn, the foremost expert on Hwang's philosophy (Hwang has said so himself in public), and his guidance, I managed to navigate through these uncharted waters. I don't pretend to understand enough to write treatises on Hwang's philosophy. I will leave that task for Sohn and other scholars to bear. I will try to relate to readers Hwang's experiences as North Korea's leading ideologue, as well as his search for a new truth in the South, in hopes that this will lead to a better understanding of North Korea and its cult of power and demigods.

October 11, 2010

I was at my home in Oakland when I received a call from a *Korea Times* reporter. He simply said, "Mr. Hwang is gone."

I was on the airplane to Korea the next day to attend the funeral for a man I'd known for seven years. During the long airplane ride to Incheon, I kept telling myself, "It's not fair, it's not fair." It wasn't fair that he should die without fulfilling what he had set out to do. He so wanted to tell the world about the corrupt regime that only was interested in perpetuating its reign on the people of North Korea.

Hwang had been a part of North Korea's ruling class over four decades, believing all the while that the proletarian dictatorship was the way. Nevertheless, in the end, his conscience would not permit him to continue to side with the brutal regime that turned its back on its own people, mainly the 3 million victims who died in one of the worst famines mankind has ever seen. He was convinced that Kim Jong-il was only interested in advancing his own causes. This led to his decision to leave his country and the people he so loved. By crossing the border, he risked everything—his life, his family, and his friends.

He wanted to find friends to work with him on improving the lives of the people in the North. He found some. Joining him in his movement to democratize North Korea are twenty thousand expatriates, his fellow defectors, and a handful of young activists from the South. Interestingly enough, his southern constituents and comrades are former Marxist sympathizers and supporters of Kim Il-sung. They discovered the true identity of the Kim regime and are following Hwang's mission to democratize North Korea.

I stand in front of Hwang's grave in Dae Jon National Cemetery, located about one hour south of Seoul, and think that he has given so much of himself for his people. I wonder if I could do what he did under the circumstances. I don't think I can. All I can do is place a white chrysanthemum in front of his grave and thank him for his courage to speak out and act on what he believed right. This book is dedicated to his efforts.

CHAPTER 1

THE SUMMIT

Kim Jong-il & Kim Dae-jung

June 13, 2000

A Boeing jet carrying South Korean president Kim Dae-jung and his presidential party swooped down on the tarmac of the Sun Ahn Airport outside Pyongyang, slowly taxied toward the concourse, and rolled to a stop, precisely in front of a reception area covered with a red carpet. Cameras zoomed in on the airplane's door in anticipation of the visiting dignitary, and the door opened. Kim Dae-jung emerged from the plane. The octogenarian smiled and waved to the roaring North Koreans, women dressed in colorful Korean garb and men in suits, all of them waving flowers and flags with unprecedented fervor. The elderly statesman gingerly climbed down the ramp, one step at a time, until he finally touched down on the red carpet.

Waiting to greet him was Kim Jong-il, the younger of the two Kims, who took the elder Kim's hands, shook them, and held them, warm and close. It could easily have been the picture of a reunion of two long-lost relatives, an uncle on a visit to his nephew's home.

"Welcome, Mr. President," Kim Jong-il said. "You're so brave to travel all this way."

The elder Kim, sometimes referred to as DJ, beamed with reckless abandon, contrary to his usual stoic demeanor, while the younger Kim assured his "uncle" that all was well in the fatherland. DJ understood what Kim Jong-il meant about being "brave" to visit Pyongyang.

Even though the flight only took one hour, the distance between them metaphysically and metaphorically was a million miles, from one end of the world to the other. They had been living as enemies for five decades, ever since the Korean War in 1950. Technically they were still at war, separated by a strip of land about a mile and a half wide, running across the peninsula's waist. It is universally called the DMZ (Demilitarized Zone), a striking misnomer, since the DMZ is the most heavily armed area in the world. Tons of missiles, tanks, and a million-plus troops are poised for a fight at a moment's notice. Countless landmines are buried in between the missiles, tanks, and troops, a testimony to lingering conflict between the North and the South. Former president Bill Clinton once visited the DMZ and called it "the scariest place on Earth."

DJ replied, "It is great to see you," and shook Kim Jong-il's hand again. DJ was surprised to see him at the airport, because the original plan had called for a meeting at the guest house. But then, Kim Jong-il was a man of surprises, and one could always count on that.

Kim Jong-il has reveled in unpredictability over the years. This summit in 2000 was his turn to shine, his time, his show for the entire world. He was ready to make the most out of this rare opportunity as the world press swarmed his city, Pyongyang. He especially liked shocking the old politician from the South, who had paid millions of dollars (reportedly $500 million, one-half the amount originally asked for) for the privilege of visiting Pyongyang under the premise of promoting peace on the peninsula. He knew that DJ aspired to go down in history as the "unification president" of the Korean Peninsula, and he meant to capitalize on what he perceived as the old man's weakness. As much as he abhorred capitalism, Kim Jong-il needed the money, and in return, he was willing to "grace" the world with his charm. The Western press had been harsh on him over the years, painting him as an isolationist dictator who purposefully starved his people while he lived in luxury and wealth in his many palaces. At the same time, it has long been evident that he didn't care what the capitalist press said about him. In his mind, they were always wrong and didn't deserve any attention. He has always touted that all the criticisms he received in the capitalist press meant that he was doing something right.

However, something strange happened during the days of the 2000 summit. Kim Jong-il had the press eating out of his hands. Their cameras recorded every moment the two Kims were together, except during the forty-minute limo ride from the airport to DJ's guest house, leaving everyone to wonder about the content of the private conversation. The reporters were enthralled with Kim Jong-il, who was wryly cracking jokes during these encounters. He said at the dinner with DJ, "In Europe, they say that I live a secluded life, but actually I have traveled quite a bit. This time, you came to liberate me from seclusion." Everyone broke out in laughter, including the reporters. He continued and asked DJ, "How is the noodle soup? The noodles don't taste good if you rush it. Please take your time and enjoy the noodles." He jumped from one subject to another, showing that he was in charge of the conversations at the table.

Kim Jong-il handled these reporters with ease. They lapped up everything he threw out, hailing him as "humorous," "honest," "well-informed," and so on. These were the same reporters who had described him as an "enigma," an "odd weirdo," a "drunken womanizer," and an "incompetent leader."

He smirked at the headline in the South's morning newspaper on June 15, the last day of the summit. It read, "Chairman Kim demonstrates his drinking ability," referring to the wine toast he had made at the dinner the night before and the way he downed a large glass of wine in one smooth gulp. Kim Jong-il said, "I don't know why they [the Southern press] take potshots at me like this."

DJ replied, "Well, it took me four sips to finish my glass."

Kim Jong-il came back with, "But they say nothing about your drinking ... just about my drinking ability. I suppose I proved to them what they suspected all along."

Laughter broke out. He waited for the laughter to subside and said, "Well, I suppose it makes for a good story."

The summit ended well as far as Kim Jong-il was concerned, a personal victory as well as a victory for the revolution. The people in the South became crazy about him. They even imitated his hairstyle and his jumpsuit. He had been under his father's shadow all his life, but thanks to this "coming out party," he showed himself as a capable leader for the whole world to see. The capitalist hype thrust him onto the international stage, and a long list of visitors came to see him in droves—South Korean businessmen, politicians, US Secretary of State Madeline Albright, myriad congressional members from the United States, representatives from the EU. That wasn't all. He had summit meetings with Chinese Premier Chiang, Russian President Putin, and Prime Minister Koizumi of Japan. Everyone wanted to meet this "changed" man, and the Western press kept him in the headlines.

While Kim was enjoying his new stature following his "coming out party," Hwang Jang-yop was quietly watching his old nemesis on television from a distance, in Seoul, South Korea. He had known Kim Jong-il as a young man and recognized his ambition for power. As Kim's mentor and advisor to his father, Kim Il-sung, Hwang saw Kim rise to the top and ultimately gain control of the country. However, his close relationship with Kim Jong-il deteriorated around 1993, when Hwang sought to reform the ailing economy by moving it toward an open-market economy styled after the Chinese model. Kim Jong-il saw the solution differently; he argued for nuclear weapons. Kim Il-sung went along with Kim Jong-il. Even though Kim Jong-il won the argument, he didn't feel comfortable because he was afraid that many party elites agreed with Hwang on reforming economic policies. Kim Jong-il ordered surveillance on Hwang and began persecuting him.

Hwang realized that he could no longer continue in his position as the general secretariat of the party and had to make the very difficult decision to defect. That was three years before the summit. Hwang wrote about these pivotal moments in his memoirs. The following is my translation of excerpts from his memoirs.[1]

> That day on January 30, 1997, I don't recall what the weather was like in Pyongyang. My memory of the city is shrouded in heavy fog under the gray sky, reflecting the state of my mind as I left home that day. My wife came out to the gate to see me off. My son Kyung-mo was away in a hospital being treated for his liver infection, and his wife and children were still asleep. As I looked at my wife—she knew nothing—I felt torn again. Should I tell her that I might never see her again?
>
> But I didn't tell her anything. I just went ahead with the decision that I had struggled with for months. I finally decided it was better not to tell her, for I was never certain if things would turn out the way I had planned. Telling her would increase the chance of compromising the secrecy by twofold, not to mention the pain she would feel. She and I had built together a life of fifty years and varied accomplishments, and my actions would be very difficult for her, even if she understood what I was doing. The thought of our shattered life would bring her great pain. Such pain would destroy her even before my defection came to fruition.
>
> "I'll be back. I should be back around February 12," I said and then parted from her after a brief farewell.
>
> We'd met in faraway Moscow during those wonderful days in our youth, followed by the half century of love and trust. I struggled over my decision endlessly, whether I should tell her about my plan, or even mention the possibility that I might not ever see her again. But, in the end, I did not let on at all.
>
> As I look back, however, I think she had an intuitive feeling about my plans. One summer day in 1996, I was in the vegetable garden in the backyard of our house in Pyongyang, thinking about the nation's fate, when she came up and asked whether I was worried about something. She did not look at me directly, her eyes fixed on the tomato

---

[1] Hwang Jang-yop, *I Witnessed the True History: Hwang Jang-yop Memoir*, Hwang Jang-yop Hoe Go Rok/Na-neun Yeoksa-ui Jinli-rul Bo ahtta,(Seoul: Shidae Jongshin, 2006).

plants. I didn't want to pass my struggles onto her, and I gave her a simple answer: no.

Then she spoke in Russian, "We've had a good life up to now. I have no regrets ... even if we were to die right away. But think about how many people depend on you. You have to be patient, if not for us, for them."

She surprised me with those words, as if she knew my plans. I replied in Russian, "A family's life is more important than an individual's life; a nation's life is more important than a family's; the human race is more important than a nation." Then I muttered something like "I have seen the truth of history," thinking that she didn't hear me. I think she heard me, though.

She turned around silently, holding the basket filled with tomatoes. The slump in her shoulders remains vivid in my memory. She might not have understood my meaning exactly, but she might have sensed that I was up to something.

There was another incident about two weeks before I departed the North. I burned two trunks full of manuscripts I had worked on. My wife quietly came up to me and asked, "Why are you burning manuscripts so dear to you?"

"I don't think I need them anymore." I made a short reply then, and she didn't pursue the topic any further. She may have thought that I could no longer publish the manuscripts because they contained banned materials.

I was somewhat relieved that she didn't press me for details. I watched my written thoughts turn to ashes, and I went in the house. Then I asked her to give away my camera, expensive pens, and other valuable things to our children. We still needed some of those things, but my wife didn't say anything. She merely followed my instructions. Did she guess what was on my mind? Was she already prepared for the hardship and sacrifice that lay ahead for her, hardships harsher than death itself?

Of course, I was most concerned with my family's welfare and attempted countless plans to arrange for their safety before I left, which, alas, proved impossible. In the meantime, I was haunted by a nagging voice inside: *If you hesitate, as you try to save your family, even though you know you can't, you'll never make the move in the end. Then history will say that there was not one intellectual who criticized or protested against the conditions in the North, the violence and the injustice that was perpetrated on my people, my fatherland.* Thus I made the decision to leave my family behind. I had to.

I had originally planned to defect in Japan, but I had to cancel it. The members of Joson Youth Party in Japan, citing security reasons, never left me alone, day or night. They stuck by my side in numbers that made me wonder if they were following a special directive from Kim Jong-il. So I decided to defect in Beijing, China, the next scheduled stop.

My actual defection began at nine in the morning on February 12, 1997. Under the guise of gift shopping, my assistant, Kim Duk-hong, and I went to a department store near the South Korean Embassy in Beijing. We met with several helpers there and discussed the details of the defection. After a brief discussion with the coordinator of our defection, we slipped out the back door of the department store and took a taxi to the South Korean Embassy, where its staff members waited for us. When we arrived, they led us to the consul general.

"Mr. Hwang, welcome, sir," the consul general said, and I held his hand without saying a word.

The South Korean Embassy in Beijing informed the Chinese Foreign Affairs Office of my defection at 11:30 in the morning. At 5:30 p.m., I was told that the South Korean government had made an official announcement.

One thing I most worried about was whether the Chinese government would allow our defection to take place on their soil. I had always loved the Chinese culture and maintained good relations with Chinese officials in my capacity as a North Korean official and a proponent of a strong alliance with China. Therefore, I had no doubt that the Chinese officials would feel favorable toward me. But in terms of national interest, China could ill afford to exchange Kim Jong-il's goodwill for me. It was a good possibility that Kim Jong-il could compel the Chinese government to return us to North Korea or send us to a third country.

On February 13, the day after I walked into the South Korean Embassy, the North Korea Ministry of Foreign Affairs announced that if South Korea had kidnapped us, it would pay an appropriate price. Then the Chinese Foreign Affairs Office announced its official position, requesting all the parties to treat the matter in accordance with international rules. I also heard that the South Korean minister of foreign affairs, Kim Ha-jung, sent a special envoy to Beijing, requesting the Chinese government's cooperation.

As it was reported in the press, several hundred North Korean agents made several attempts to penetrate through the Chinese police to get at us. However, they failed to reach us inside the South Korean Embassy, owing to the protection provided by the Chinese, with 1,200 armed police and a tank reinforcing the perimeter.

I had no doubt in my mind what those agents were after; they had stormed the Russian Embassy in Pyongyang and assassinated a military officer who had defected there some years ago. The South Korean Embassy officials, realizing the potential danger, intensified their effort.

I was not myself during these few crucial days. But as soon as I heard that the Chinese government expressed its intention to cooperate with the South Korean government with regard to my defection, I relaxed. Then I began to worry about my family. The worried faces of my wife and children kept appearing in front of me, and I couldn't sleep, even with the help of sleeping pills. I would get up and take another sleeping pill in order to get any sleep at all. I was simply going insane. I buried the family photograph deep in my trunk to avoid looking at them, thinking about them. But I couldn't bury the images that popped up in my head all the time, day and night. My longing multiplied, especially at mealtimes. The embassy personnel learned that I liked candy, and they brought candy for me now and then.... I was besieged with my grandson Ji-sung's image, the way he opened his mouth saying, "Ah, ah," asking me to drop one in his mouth. I couldn't swallow the candy then. Ji-sung would always come to me at the dinner table and ask me to feed him. Had I been able to go back to Pyongyang then, I would have taken the candies for Ji-sung.

In the meantime, we waited for the Chinese government and its next move. Our fate hung on their decision—although it seemed unlikely that they would ship me back to North Korea. The South Korean Embassy staff had a variety of opinions with respect to what China might do. Some were hopeful that the Chinese government would handle our defection according to the international rules and regulations, while others feared that the Chinese government would just keep us in limbo.

I asked them how long the Chinese government could drag things on, and they replied, "Six months to a year." They added, "But the South Korean Embassy is South Korean territory, and the Chinese government cannot drag you out of here by force."

I resolved to wait it out in the South Korean Embassy for six months to a year until my journey to South Korea became a reality. If my defection failed, I decided that I would take my own life. It so happened that I had acquired a cyanide pill in Pyongyang, and I had tucked it in my breast pocket and kept it there. Oddly, this simple act gave me a sense of comfort, purging all my angst and even reinvigorating me.

★★★

The Chinese government did not return Hwang to North Korea. Instead, they allowed Hwang and his assistant, Kim Duk-hong, to depart from China to a third country, the Philippines. Hwang and Kim stayed in the Philippines for a month and finally made their way to Seoul on April 20, 1997.

His arrival in the South made a huge splash in the news. As it so often happens with events in Korea, his arrival was politicized to the hilt. He was billed as the highest-ranking official ever to defect from North Korea, someone with deep secrets from the inner circles of the Northern hierarchy. He was reported to have in his possession a list of Northern implants of the highest order among the rank and file within the South Korean government. The so-called "Hwang Jang-yop's List" received a great deal of attention from the press, heralded as the bombshell that would turn the administration upside down. But the list never existed. Hwang told me it was a product of the imagination of some unscrupulous sensationalists from the press.

Worse yet, many people questioned his motivation—how could he abandon his family, knowing the plight that was sure to befall them? Abandoning one's family was beyond people's imagination, no matter what the cause. It was too much to ask an average person to understand his mission to solve the starvation problem and to forewarn the world about the senseless rise of militarism in the North. History has proven that combination of a failing economy and expanding militarism make for a formula for certain disaster, and Hwang meant to prevent this impending doom in the Korean Peninsula. But to his amazement, he found himself in a struggle to prove his own credibility, especially among the scholars and experts in the South. "The so-called experts have very little or no understanding of the realities in the North," Hwang pointed out to me, "yet they insist on their own brand of truth. It is exasperating."

When he had spoken of the widespread famine and given them his estimate of 3 million deaths, they did not believe the numbers. Hwang wrote, "In November 1996, I asked the chief of the statistics bureau about the number of deaths. He told me that in 1995 there were approximately 500,000 deaths, including 50,000 Party members. He said that 1996 would bring about one million deaths. He also predicted two million deaths in 1997 in the event that there was no outside help."

He told this to various officials and experts in the South, as well as the American experts, but perhaps these numbers were too appalling for anyone to comprehend. It took a long time for Hwang to convince the powers that be in the South that there was a serious problem. He also asserted that there was need for a fundamental change in the economic and political system in the North, in order to save the population from further starvation. The fundamental change meant the privatization of farmlands and the creation of an open-market system, which, of course, Kim Jong-il opposed.

Hwang, as the chairman of the Foreign Relations Committee of the Party, in addition to his post as the general secretariat, had a clear view of the economic situation in the region. It made no sense to him that North Korea, surrounded by such robust economies as Japan, China, and South Korea, should suffer such a catastrophe. He wrote in his memoirs:[2]

> That year [1995], the food situation worsened every day. But rather than solving the food crisis, Kim Jong-il solidified his dictatorship. He reinforced the secret police and, if there was any indication of anti-state activities, he sought out the leaders and shot them openly or discreetly, without a trial. Once, one of my guards came up to me and quietly told me, "There are monitoring devices in your office. They can hear and see everything you do. Please be careful."

---

[2] Ibid.

Kim Jong-il's solution to the food crisis was to declare the "Arduous March," modeled after Kim Il-sung's campaign against the Japanese military during the 1930s. In early January 1995, Kim Jong-il assembled his top officials and made the following announcement:

> I have devised a motto called, "The Arduous March." This is from Su Ryong-nim's [Kim Il-sung] lofty revolutionary ideals that he used in leading our anti-Japan struggles during the time when conditions were much worse than it is today. You shall lead your lives in the spirit of the "Arduous March" as well.

With these words, Hwang recognized and understood that the food crisis was going to worsen before it got better, because the "Arduous March" was not logical. He knew that what the country needed was food, not a test to see how long humans could go without it. Already there were reports of starvation in the countryside and parts of Pyongyang. The energy crisis was worsening too. It was so bad that even the goldfish at the office of the Party Central froze to death.

Hwang relentlessly advocated adopting an open-market system styled after the Chinese model, but to no avail. Some of Hwang's followers also began talking about reforming the economy, and no doubt that information reached Kim Jong-il's ears, which most likely explains the close scrutiny Hwang was subjected to during this period.

Kim Jong-il was dead set against such economic reform, which we can glean from his so-called "Kim Il-sung University Speech" in December of 1996. [3]

> On the way to the *Chollima* Steel factory, I saw along the roadway a line of people searching for food. I also saw crowds of people looking for food in other areas as well. I hear that trains are also filled with people in search of food. We have endured bad crops three years in a row now, and we are surviving on international aid.... Our country is suffering from the lack of food. We don't have rice for the military. Our country is in a state of anarchy because of the dysfunctional food rationing system. The administration department is

---

[3] K.J. Sohn, *Kim Jong-il Report* (Seoul: Bada Publishing, 2003), p.181, excerpt translated by John Cha

responsible for this mess, as well as the Party officials. The Party's Central Committee members have failed their duty in generating a revolutionary spirit, diminishing the Party's effectiveness. We must solve the food problem according to socialist principles, and must not rely on individuals. If we let the people solve the problem on their own, only merchants and markets will prosper. Then, selfishness will rule our society and destroy our system of true equality.

The complexity of world politics today precludes me from taking on additional duties of dealing with domestic economy and its problems. I must focus all my energy on the important tasks concerning the Party and the military.... SuRyong-nim has repeated to me several times that I would be unable to take care of the affairs of the Party or the military if I were dragged into matters of economy.

We can gather from this speech that he was aware of the food problem and that he blamed everyone else for the dire situation. His reference to a "state of anarchy" was a startling acknowledgement of a sinking ship that he was in charge of, and yet he was trying to remove himself from responsibility. Hwang was alarmed. He proposed economic reform and continued to speak up for reform, and that put him on a collision course with Kim Jong-il.

Hwang said in a press interview upon his defection, "Socialist principles are dead. People are starving to death," directing a salvo at Kim Jong-il.

Kim Jong-il said at a later date, "Regarding the open-door policy, I have already done all of the door-opening and reforming that need to be done. So, there is no more reform or opening to be done in our country. All we need are strict rules in all the workplaces and to continue to construct our own socialist state. The most important element in building our own socialist state is the military."

So when Hwang watched Kim perform as the witty leader on television on June 15, 2000, to the delight of the members of the international press, he knew Kim had become a two-headed monster, mad yet brilliant; this was the young man he had mentored and watched grow up. South Koreans were hanging on to his words like they were gold, thinking that his words marked the beginning of a real peace and unification. But Hwang knew better. As far as he was concerned, the summit was nothing but a charade, a complete bust.

Hwang told me in an interview in 2008, "Kim Jong-il doesn't want any change. He would rather sacrifice 3 million people than give up his control. His father, Kim Il-sung, had a genuine concern for the people [of North Korea]. He would never let people starve the way Kim Jong-il has. Kim Jong-il is indifferent. He would start a war if he was sure of victory. But he knows too well that he couldn't win. That is precisely why he doesn't start it. He is faithful to his own interest. He will only do something when it is beneficial for him. He has a talent for subjugating people. He knows how to manipulate people and is very skillful in elevating them and crushing them. I have watched him take over the Party and the military under the most difficult circumstances; he knows how to seize power and hold it. He is a capable dictator who doesn't value or love people. He is cruel, a tyrannical egoist. Like all tyrants, he is also very intelligent and a habitual liar. Kim knows the value of propaganda. That is why he has people refer to him as 'fatherland.' It may sound absurd, but people will become used to the word and title if you train them over and over. They accept it after a while, forgoing any analysis. Joseph Goebbels, propaganda director from the Nazi era, said that if you repeat something three times, while you choke off all other thoughts, people will believe white lies. He said, 'If you tell a lie big enough and keep repeating it, people will eventually come to believe it.' From early on, Kim Jong-il thought it was important to seize information because of this principle—that once you secure information, you can control fate. He has always organized everything in secret and executed the plan in secret. That is his specialty."

CHAPTER 2
KIM JONG-IL'S YOUTH

⸻⸺⸻

EARLY DAYS

Hwang's insight about Kim Jong-il comes from years of observation up close. Hwang felt imperative that the free world accurately understand Kim and his background if they were to deal with him. Here are some salient facts about Kim's origin.

February 16, 1942

> *It was a clear, cloudless morning. Pristine, white snow covered the remote village nestled among the thick forest, hidden from the Japanese imperialist army. The first cry of the new-born echoed throughout the base, and all the commandos rushed out of their log cabins to share the news with everyone else. Right then the sun rose and they gathered under the red flag fluttering like a flame in the morning sun. They blessed the baby's future—bright as the sun—and prayed for the liberation of the fatherland.* [4]

---

[4] Translated by John Cha, an excerpt from *General Kim Jong-il, Our Guiding Sun*, Hyangdo-ui Tae Yahng Kim Jong-il Jahng Goon, edited by Jang Seok, Ri Ju-cheol, (Pyongyang: Pyongyang Publishing, 1995)

This was the story Kim Jong-il's mother and her partisan compatriots had told him over and over—that he was born in the BaikDu Mountains, an ancient volcanic mountain revered by all Koreans as a holy place where the original founder of the Korean nation, Dangun, hailed from five thousand years ago. His mother had said to the young Kim Jong-il, "You were born in Mil Young, deep in the BaikDu Mountains. That was your father's command post for his partisan guerrillas against the Japanese army. We were always cold and starved, but we fought hard. And the Japanese feared us. When you grow up, you will be by your father's side and help him with our liberation and revolution. He is a great man. You will have to carry on your father's work someday."

During those early years, Kim was too young to understand words like *liberation* and *revolution,* and before she could explain herself, or before he was old enough to understand her, she passed away. He was eight years old, and she was thirty-two. Although they didn't spend much time together, she nevertheless had a tremendous impact on his life. He would often say, "I owe everything to my mother."

Kim Jong-il's mother, Kim Jong-sook, was born in HoeRyung, North HamKyung Province, on December 24, 1919. She went to Jilin Province (formerly a region in Manchuria in northeastern China) with her family when she was five years old but became separated from her family sometime later. When she was sixteen, she joined Kim Il-sung's partisan guerrilla unit and cooked and washed for the troops. An excellent rifle shot, Kim Jong-sook was known to have saved Kim Il-sung's life. That was reason enough for a commando named Choi Hyun to nudge Kim Il-sung into marrying her. Kim Tong-kyu, one of Kim Il-sung's men, described the life of the newlyweds at the time:

> They dug a hole in the ground large enough to crawl in. Then they started a fire with bush clover branches. When the fire died down, they scooped away the ashes and spread a fur blanket in the hole and lay down. It was toasty and warm even in the bitter cold winter—just like the lower end of the *ondol* floor of a rich house.

Thus they began their life as man and wife under the direst of circumstances, in the middle of the most confusing period of time in the Korean Peninsula. The Great War was in full swing in Europe and the Pacific Ocean. In Far East Asia, Imperial Japan had its grip on the Korean Peninsula and Manchuria, while Mao's communist forces in China were marching against the nationalist China as well as the Japanese forces. Kim Il-sung's guerrilla regiment, once attached to the communist Chinese army, now belonged to the Soviet Fareast Division.

Forty days after his birth, Kim Jong-il's mother left him at a Russian nursery and returned to her partisan duties, which was typical for partisan women at that time. His mother and her friend would go to the nursery to nurse their respective children in between commando training, and often her friend ended up nursing Kim Jong-il because his mother didn't produce enough milk.

Kim Jong-il with his parents

As a youngster, Kim Jong-il went by the name of Yura (an affectionate term for *Yuri*), given to him by a Russian friend in Habvrosk. Yura, an introvert, played mostly with his childhood friend Sergey Lee, whose father was one of Kim Il-sung's commandos. The two families were close, and Yura and Sergey were inseparable, especially because Yura (not yet fluent in Korean) and Sergey spoke Russian to each other.

Yura followed his mother to Pyongyang in November 1945 and entered Namsan Kindergarten, an exclusive school for the children of high government officials. By this time, he had a younger brother by the name of Shura (Kim Man-il), born the year before in 1944. His sister, Kyoung-hui, would follow in 1946.

Yura liked to dress up in his military uniform, and sometimes he would march around the yard and around the pond. In the summer of 1947, he and Shura were playing near the pond when Shura drowned to death.

Tragedy struck again in 1949, when he lost his mother while she was giving birth to a stillborn fetus in September. She was thirty-two. Yura had entered Namsan Elementary School just a few months before. It is difficult to discern how these early losses impacted young Yura. There is no reliable material available regarding this aspect of his formative years. However, biographies published in North Korea describe his elementary school days in glowing terms—telling how he was a bright, talented child and a hard worker. He was considered a top student and displayed tremendous leadership capabilities.

Yura and his sister Kyoung-hui grew up very close. With the advent of the Korean War in June 1950, Yura and Kyoung-hui stayed with a relative while their father was busy running the war. When the tide of the war turned against the North Korean People's Army, their uncle Kim Young-ju took them to Jilin in Manchuria. Yura stayed there for two years, attending Jilin Academy. He briefly attended ManGyungDae Revolutionary Academy, which was established on behalf of the children of those commandos who had served under Kim Il-sung's partisan unit. It should be noted that many of its graduates are currently high government officials in North Korea.

Yura returned to Pyongyang after the war and completed his elementary schooling at Pyongyang Fourth Elementary School in August 1954. It was about this time when his father married again, to Kim Song-ae.

Born on a farm in 1928, Kim Song-ae joined the army shortly before the Korean War began and worked as a secretary in Premier Kim Il-sung's office. Sixteen years younger than Kim Il-sung, she was attractive and intelligent. He needed someone to look after his children while he attended to the affairs of state, such as rebuilding the country that had been decimated by the endless bombing during the war. He felt comfortable that she would do a good job caring for Yura and Kyoung-hui.

She did her best to treat them like royalty, but she was always an outsider as far as Yura was concerned, and so were the three children she later had with Kim Il-sung: Pyong-il, Young-il, and Kyung-jin. Yura resented her. He resented his father for bringing her into their house—*no strange woman was going to take his mother's place.*

17

MIDDLE AND HIGH SCHOOL DAYS

Following his graduation from the elementary school, Yura went to Pyongyang First Middle School. His official biography describes him as a brilliant student in his middle school, demonstrating his superb intelligence in his classroom. In truth, Yura was never one to concentrate on his books for very long, which made him a mediocre student. Hwang affirmed this about Kim. "He didn't have the patience to finish a book, nor did he have the patience to solve a math problem." Kim's father was aware of this and was concerned. He often invited Yura's teachers to the family residence.

One day, Kim Il-sung invited Yura's homeroom teacher over for dinner. As the teacher arrived, Kim Il-sung had Yura come with him to the front gate to greet the teacher, which seemed extraordinary. His father was the premier, and his teacher was just a teacher, after all. Yet his father went out of his way to show respect for the teacher. In addition, his father, a nonsmoker himself, even offered a cigarette to the teacher. Yura was astounded that his father would go that far to please his teacher.

Their conversation moved on to his studies. The teacher asked Yura, "How much homework have you done today?"

Yura hesitated, unsure of what the homework assignments were. Kim Il-sung said, "Teacher, I apologize. From now on, please stop by at least once a month. I'm glad that you visited us today. Now I know what's going on."

Kim Il-sung was afraid that Yura was getting a big head because he was the premier's son, which was adversely affecting his study habits. Kim Il-sung had an intense interest in Yura's education. He took his summer vacation at Yak Su-ri every year. He always took Yura with him and practiced speaking Russian, to make sure that Yura didn't forget the language he had learned as a youngster. Kim Il-sung spoke fluent Russian and Chinese.

One year during a winter break, he tested Yura's language skills that they had worked on together the previous summer. Yura did poorly, and his father became angry. "You have been studying Russian every day, but you are a terrible speaker. What did you learn at school?"

Yura replied, "Yes, we study Russian a lot at school, but nothing stays with me."

"That's because you don't study, right?"

"I do study, but ..." Yura didn't answer his father.

When they returned home from the break, Kim Il-sung called the minister of education into his office and ordered a review of the Russian language program, especially the conversational skills taught at Namsan School. A review committee was promptly organized, and the committee found that the language teachers were quite capable and their teaching methods were high caliber. The teachers were either born in Russia or had studied there. The problem was Yura's laziness, not the teachers. Nevertheless, the committee decided to change the teachers because of Kim Il-sung's order to improve the language program. While he struggled with his studies, Yura was selected as the president of the boys' club during his second year in middle school, and that was the highlight of his time at his middle school.

At his high school, he was picked as the vice president (under a faculty president) of the youth alliance group. He attended Namsan High School, which was set up for the children of high officials, specifically those of deputy minister level and above. Students from an average home were not admitted. Should a student's father lose his post, he was required to transfer his child or children to a regular school.

The Namsan School was an elite school with the best of instructors and facilities, all focused on producing future leaders. There was another underlying reason for building a separate, elite school: they wanted to avoid the risk of information leakage via the children on matters associated with the Party and the military.

As a high school student, Yura was interested in soccer, fishing, and hunting. He also liked to ride motorcycles and drive fast cars. His personality changed about this time as well. He was no longer the introvert. His high school classmates remember that he made friends easily and was open to everyone. He often took in movies, dance performances, and music concerts with his friends, followed by parties at his home.

He became involved in school activities, organizing anti-America demonstrations, the graduation yearbook, and the graduation party. He tackled everything with heart. That was his style.

Considering his proclivity for these extracurricular activities during high school, it is doubtful that he was as brilliant a student as his official biography claims. Yet, despite his haphazard efforts in schoolwork, Yura really couldn't do anything wrong in his father's eyes.

The truth of the matter was that Yura was more interested in his father. In January 1959, Yura, then seventeen years old, accompanied his father on a trip to Moscow for the Twenty-First Communist Party Congress of the Soviet Union. He did not, however, attend any of the events, staying back at the hotel on many occasions. More than the congress, he was interested in looking after his father. Every morning, when his father was getting ready to go out, Yura would help his father by holding him up by his arm. He even helped his father put on his shoes.

Now, Kim Il-sung was forty-seven years old, full of energy, and he didn't need any assistance. But he always enjoyed his son's gestures. When Kim Il-sung came back in the evening, Yura brought together all the assistants, the doctor, and the nurse, and asked for a report on the day's events. Then he gave them instructions on matters dealing with his father's health and security. He even gave detailed instructions to the politicos from the Central Party on matters of state, which was well beyond Yura's purview. Nevertheless, the men from the Central Party quietly listened to the youngster. As Hwang Jang-yop watched Yura instruct the men, he thought that Yura was not an ordinary boy but an ambitious young man who knew how to exercise his power.

The following summer, 1960, as he was about to graduate from high school, he told his classmates one day, "I am no longer Kim Yura. I've changed my name to Kim Jong-il, so call me by my new name from now on."

There seems to be a political motivation behind the name change. His father was openly critical of Khrushchev at that time, charging that the Soviet premier was a revisionist for reaching out to the Western bloc. Khrushchev was tearing down Stalin's statues as well, and Kim Il-sung was very upset that Stalin, his mentor, would suffer such a disgrace. But more importantly, Kim Il-sung was establishing a new direction for North Korea, busily positioning himself between China and the USSR, playing the two powers against each other for his own gain. It would have been inappropriate for his son to continue using his Russian name under the circumstances, and so Kim Il-sung ordered the name change.

UNIVERSITY DAYS

On September 1, 1960, Kim Jong-il enrolled in Kim Il-sung University's School of Economics, majoring in political economics. Being the most elite institution for higher learning, only the top students were admitted. The students' family background was also an important consideration at that time, and sometimes academic standards were a secondary condition for those children of the high officials.

The crop of university students of the 1960s is referred to as the "*Chollima* Generation." These students took an active part in the *Chollima* Movement, a six-year economic plan instituted by Kim Il-sung. It was more than an economic plan for increasing GNP, however. In addition to the economic revival, the plan was to increase awareness among the masses and the workers about the communist ethos. More importantly, the movement was an opportunity for the Party to assert its principles to its members, the farmers, and factory workers. The plan worked well. Here's a testimony by a former professor:[5]

> At the height of the *Chollima* Movement during the 1960s, there was no such thing as a thief. People didn't lock their doors. We helped each other and lived together as one big family. If a neighbor became ill, everyone rushed to help, brought food, didn't spare anything. If a couple got into an argument, their neighbors helped them resolve their issues as if the conflict was their own. Once, a family suffered a fire. The news went out, and people gathered in front of the hospital and stood in line to volunteer themselves for the skin graft operations and transfusions. The Rodong Sinmun covered the story extensively, together with many photographs. North Korea was a good place to live in the 1960s.

Kim Jong-il spent his college days at the height of the *Chollima* era, involved in on-the-job training and military training, in addition to his classroom work. He went to work at a textile machinery manufacturing facility in Pyongyang and worked as a laborer for a road expansion project.

---

[5]   Interview conducted by K.J. Sohn with a former professor of Kim Il-sung University, who had defected from North Korea. He chose to remain anonymous.

As the son of the premier, he had special privileges. Fellow students didn't refer to him by his name, but as the "premier's son." He had a special advisor by the name of Kim In-sook, a professor in the history department. She was responsible for setting up Kim Jong-il's curriculum and arranging private tutors in the subjects of politics, economics, history, philosophy, and Russian. His private tutors were top specialists in their respective fields. As his college days wore on, he didn't work at the construction sites anymore. Instead he participated in party conferences, cabinet meetings, and other government functions. He was also active in the student chapter of the Workers' Party.

One of his most notable accomplishments at the university was the initiation of a reading program that required everyone to read ten thousand pages of books a year. It is not clear whether Kim Jong-il himself actually read ten thousand pages of books each and every year, but this program later developed into the "10,000 Pages-per-Year Reading Initiative" for the Kim Il-sung Socialist Youth Alliance, which mainly involved reading about Kim Il-sung. What began as an initiative in the Economics Department became a university-wide movement, and then a national effort at all the colleges and universities.

For his graduation thesis, Kim Jong-il wrote a paper entitled, "Building Socialism: The Position and the Role of the State." In the paper, he cites the importance of upgrading the farm communities to the administrative status of cities and the role the counties should play in this effort. The paper was brilliant. It ought to have been—it was written by Chon Yong-sik, Kim Jong-il's economics professor. According to Hwang, Kim Jong-il didn't have the mind or patience to write an academic paper.

Kim Jong-il participated in military training for two months between his second and third year of college. His training ground has been designated as a "Revolutionary Historical Site." There is a plaque lauding Kim Jong-il's military acumen—"Just two months of training, Kim Jong-il mastered the military tactics and guided other students in learning real-time battle tactics and leadership skills."

But a close relative of Kim Sung-ae and a former officer in the People's Army suggests otherwise:[6]

---

[6] K.J. Sohn, *Kim Jong-il Report,* (Seoul: Bada Publishing, 2003), p.47, excerpt translated by John Cha

Kim Jong-il's uncle Kim Young-ju was always covering up for Kim Jong-il. His uncle, then the head of the Party's organizational guidance department, received a report that Kim Jong-il had bolted from the military base and left for somewhere unknown. His uncle pushed everything aside for the day and set out to look for Kim Jong-il before the news got to his father, Kim Il-sung.

One of the search teams spotted Kim Jong-il at the Central Film Distribution Center, where he had been watching foreign movies all day long.

His uncle brought Kim Jong-il to his office and gave him a severe beating and afterwards, brought him to the military base and handed him over to the commanding officer.

During the same training period, Kim Jong-il carved a mandolin out of a tree, which is on display at the Revolutionary Historical Site. These events indicate that his heart wasn't in the military tactics, although he was interested in target shooting. He often practiced shooting at a weapons repair center and continued to practice after his graduation at a rifle range under the direction of sharp-shooters like Lee Ho-joon and Kim Chang-ho. Lee Ho-joon won a gold medal in the Montreal Olympics in 1976 and became Kim Jong-il's personal bodyguard in 1980.

Movies were Kim's main interest during his college days. He routinely stopped in at the Central Film Distribution Center, the two-story building that was located between the Pyongyang railroad station and Botong Gate among all the Russian-style apartment buildings built right after the Korean War.

The manager at the Central Film Distribution Center first thought that Kim Jong-il had merely a passing interest in movies, a curious movie buff, never imagining that he would spend days and nights poring over foreign films in the theater. Eventually, the manager ended up providing a separate viewing room for Kim's exclusive use.

Young Kim Jong-il saw in these films a new world, his means to connect with the outside and procure knowledge and information. His interest in movies persisted, despite criticism by those who had carefully arranged his college curriculum. As it turned out, Kim knew exactly what he was doing. He understood the value of the mass media and would later use the film as the basis for his quest for power, which he would eventually inherit from his father.

Dubbed as "Operation No. 100" (Kim came up with the codename in the 1970s), his film "distribution" project involved the cooperation of various North Korean embassies in Austria, China, and Macao. These embassies and others were equipped with professional dubbing equipment to copy films for shipment to Pyongyang. Yi Jong-mok, then the first deputy foreign minister, supervised the overall operation to acquire Hollywood movies, South Korean films, Chinese kung fu films, and Japanese ninja films, among others. Once the films arrived in the Pyongyang studio, the translation team went to work on them, and the actors followed up with voiceovers in Korean. The finished production was delivered to his residence or retreat, regardless of where he might have been at the time. (Kim's personal film library consisted of fifteen thousand films from all over the world. He kept hundreds of South Korean films in a separate library, some of which were the original copies that he had acquired via Hong Kong during the 1970s. He had about 250 employees managing the library: actors, translators, subtitle makers, and dubbing experts. There was even an acquisition manager who traveled overseas to acquire Western films and shipped them through the diplomatic pouch, mainly via Moscow.)

After his graduation in 1964, his first job was with the secretarial staff of the Workers' Party Central Committee. The committee is significant because the country is structured in a unique three-tier system—the Party, the military, and the executive department, in that order. The Party is the policymaker, with the Central Committee at its heart. Everything flows from the Party, and its members are omnipresent in every facet of the military and government, as well as factories, schools, farms, and commercial entities, to make sure that all the Party edicts are complied with. Party members report all the activities back to the Central Committee, which Kim Il-sung presided over as its chairman.

This was where Kim Jong-il positioned himself, giving him a bird's-eye view of the overall makeup of the country. Kim Young-ju, his uncle and the head of the Party's Organizational Guidance Department, taught Kim Jong-il the inner workings of the Central Committee. It didn't take Kim Jong-il very long to understand the vast powers that the department wielded—control over the personnel matters in all the key positions, the power to inspect all the departments and censure them, and the power to execute Party policies.

Equally important was the Information Department that oversaw the education and indoctrination process related to matters on ideology. On a scale of importance, however, the Organizational Guidance Department precedes the Information Department. Together, they represent the real power apparatus for the Party.

After one year of service at the Party headquarters, Kim Jong-il moved to the cabinet as a staff member in the Executive Department. He carried out tasks that were specifically ordered by the Party, such as the hiring and firing of personnel, food distribution, and housing allotment. He was there for a year, rounding out his training program at both ends of the power spectrum.

Hence he was assigned to a post called the "Workers' Party Central Committee/Organizational Guidance Department/Leader-on-Duty, Central Headquarters, Instruction Section." On the surface, the job didn't seem significant. But it was, considering that he was only twenty-four years old at the time. To begin with, his affiliation with the Central Committee gave him and his staff the authority to oversee—or meddle with—the local wards within the Party's network of leaders in Pyongyang, or the Pyong An Province, for example. The Party network was quite extensive, to say the least, ranging from the Central Committee, Pyongyang, the provinces, counties, cities, villages, neighborhoods, streets, factories, farms, co-ops, and schools of all levels, all the way down to individual cells. Besides, he was the son of the premier, and no one in the hierarchy of the leaders dared to question his authority. Between 1964 and 1966, he accompanied his father on no less than thirty-one trips around the country for onsite inspection and instruction, including fifteen extended trips.

During these trips, Kim Jong-il was able to observe his father at work, inspecting factories and farms and dispensing his instructions on *Chollima* principles as well as specific directives on how to improve production for farms and factories. Kim Jong-il displayed his penchant for doling out his own instructions, as he had shown as a high school student during the Moscow trip, on matters following up on those of his father, and making sure those instructions were complied with, no matter how minute the detail. He was quick and clever, a force to be reckoned with as he gained a foothold in the Central Committee, and people referred to him as "Comrade Kim Jong-il, the Instructor."

He was well on his way to establishing his own identity beyond that of the "premier's son." He was near the bottom of the totem pole, though, nowhere near the political stage that he coveted. At this point, all he could do was bide his time.

His opportunity came in September 1967. This was a confusing period of time, caused by an ideological struggle within the Party. As mentioned earlier, the *Chollima* Movement and Kim Il-sung's economic plan proved successful, and the country was relatively prosperous, more so than the South. Kim Il-sung's plan, however, focused on heavy industries that were geared toward military applications, and the so-called Kapsan faction of the Party proposed to shift the emphasis toward non-military spending, in an effort to further improve the lives of the people. This touched off a fierce debate. The Kapsan faction further argued that the Party should rely on expert economists, scientists, and engineers to better manage the country's economy, and that the Party should reduce its role in these areas.

For example, they wanted to give more say to trained factory managers on matters of production and overall operations and take away the operational control from the presiding political officer. For Kim Il-sung and his camp, this concept was beyond comprehension, completely irresponsible. The presence of political (ideological) officers in every factory, farm, neighborhood, village, city, and school was the way of life, the means to maintain the founding ideals of the Workers' Party, and therefore, the quality of life itself. Eliminating or reducing the role of the ideological officer from the factory meant that there would be moral corruption and counter-revolution.

Apparently, Kim Il-sung strongly felt the Kapsan faction and their ideas represented a danger to the country. So dangerous in fact, Kim Il-sung ultimately purged the Party of faction members and "liberal" thinkers.

In addition to this ideological struggle, another struggle involving the selection of Kim Il-sung's successor preceded this purge. Kim Il-sung had positioned his brother, Kim Young-ju, as his successor, and the members of the Kapsan faction objected. They favored Pak Kum-chol, then the vice premier, over Kim Young-ju, against Kim Il-sung's plan. Pak was the leader of the liberal faction who sought to change the direction of the country.

To make matters worse, the Kapsan faction, in their effort to enhance Pak's image, produced a movie about him. It presented Pak as a true hero, exaggerating his accomplishments. This did not sit well with Kim Il-sung at all. The faction had garnered the support of the filmmakers and sought to take advantage of their popularity among the filmmakers to advance their liberal agenda.

All this was happening during Mao Zedong's Cultural Revolution in China in 1966. Kim Il-sung didn't support the Cultural Revolution. In fact, he criticized the movement and the purging of the Chinese intelligentsia as "revisionist." Yet he did not hesitate to take advantage of the tide of the time and carry out his own kind of political purge with the blessing of the Party members at a secret meeting in March 1967.

These officials determined at the same meeting that there could be only one ethos for the Party and the state, giving birth to the "monolithic system." According to Hwang, Kim Il-sung said, "Establishing the monolithic system is fundamental in building our Party. Without a complete monolithic system, we cannot maintain our uniform ideological identity, nor can we carry out our revolution." He continued, "I heard that in the Jagang Province and North Pyong An Province, people were studying the instructions given by the Vice Premier, and in another region, people were talking about the teachings of a manager in the Party Central. This is improper development as it goes against the principles of the monolithic system."

Subsequently on May 25, Kim Il-sung made a speech entitled "Regarding the Transition Period from Capitalism to Socialism and Issues of Proletarian Dictatorship" in front of the Party's Ideology Department personnel. There, he asserted that this transitional period, from capitalism to socialism, must be resolved with an ethos of self-reliance. This was the "May 25 Teaching," solidifying Kim Il-sung's monolithic system. It marked the beginning of a new era in North Korea—Kim Il-sung's way or no way.

Sung Hye-rang, Kim Jong-il's former sister-in-law, wrote in her memoirs:[7]

> The "May 25 Teaching" doesn't refer to the Kapsan-pa purge among the elite members of the Central Committee. I remember it as the elimination of the intelligentsia and a total attack on their cultural creativity, all in the name of the anti-revisionist movement.

---

[7] Sung Hye-rang, *Wisteria House*, Deung Namu Jip (Seoul: Jishik Nara, 2000). Sung Hye-rim's older sister and writer, Hye-rang defected in 1996.

All the North Korean people say that things were good during the 1960s. To be exact, it was a decent socialist country for the people up to the point of the "May 25 Teaching." Society came under siege by a storm from the extreme left and fervor to idolize Kim Il-sung as the Su Ryong [the supreme leader].

With the establishment of Kim Il-sung's monolithic ideology as the system, the people were urged to burn their book collections or donate them to libraries. All the books written by authors like Shakespeare, Tolstoy, Dostoevsky, and Gorky were incinerated, along with books related to Greek, Chinese, and German philosophy.

Books on Marx disappeared from library shelves about this time as well. People could read Marx only in a few select libraries, and scholars had to produce a reason for reading him. Censorship intensified in every level of the society—at home, work, and school. The North Korean version of the Cultural Revolution went further than literature or philosophy. Victims of the revolution included Soviet songs and traditional Korean music. They shattered Beethoven's busts and Venus statues and tore up Western paintings. Painters were banished to farms to do hard labor.

The winds of this purge blew across the fields of science and technology as well. Foreign technologies were rejected as revisionist. Anyone showing interest in advanced technology was criticized and ostracized.

It was in this chaotic environment that Kim Jong-il saw his opportunity. Six months into the purge, there was an unscheduled meeting at the movie studio with the Party's political committee. At this meeting, Kim Il-sung severely criticized the movie about Pak Kum-chul and exhorted, "Clean up the anti-Party elements in the field of film arts." Then he told the attendants, "I want your opinions on how to advance the film arts as a revolutionary art for the Party."

Right then someone said, "I will take on the responsibility and try it."

Everyone turned and saw Kim Jong-il. Movies were his specialty and passion, after all. And so he was promoted to cultural arts director of the Information Department right away. He was also charged with overseeing the publishing department as well, which put him in the middle of the Party's power structure. He was twenty-five years old.

For the next two years, until he became the chief of the Information Department, Kim Jong-il concentrated on projects related to the idolization of Kim Il-sung, in direct competition with his uncle. Kim Jong-il distinguished himself by utilizing cultural arts as his means for getting his father's attention and trust.

First he gathered all the actors, writers, directors, singers, musicians, and artists in the Party's auditorium and held a month-long conference on the subject of ideological struggles. The purpose of the session was to purge the art world of all the "anti-Party poison" that the Kapsan faction had injected into the system. For an entire month, the participating artists reflected on their past mistakes and engaged in self-criticism. They anticipated that they would be sent off to farms or labor camps for their misplaced loyalty and waited for the other shoe to drop.

Kim Jong-il had other plans in mind, however. He told them, "Let's do our best to repay Su Ryong-nim's kindness with our artistic endeavor and loyalty."

Stunned artists looked up to Kim Jong-il with new admiration. Kim Jong-il had them where he wanted them. They were his to do with as he wanted. They saw him as a generous, understanding person and pledged their loyalty to Kim Il-sung, the Su Ryong.

Next, Kim Jong-il modernized the movie studio. He imported the latest equipment from the Soviet Union and Europe and expanded the facility. In the meantime, he sent talented actors and directors to the Soviet Union to study. He imported a large volume of films from overseas and critiqued them with writers, directors, actors, and composers. He installed the artists as members of the Workers' Party and built a department store dedicated for their use. He provided a commuter bus for them and showered them with gifts, clothes, food, watches, record players, and television sets.

Notwithstanding the gifts and royal treatment, the artists were moved by Kim's dedication to the art and his long hours at the studio, day after day. He practically lived there. He often organized athletic events for the cultural artists, even a soccer team called "Young-hwa" (Film).

As a result, the artists developed a genuine affection for him; they coined the title "Comrade Leader" for him, a title that would spread throughout the country.

He also founded a writers' group called "The April 15th Creative Group," comprised of noted novelists, Kim Byung-hoon, Baek In-joon, and Sok Yoon-ki, the elite group of writers who put together stories for movies.

Revolution Forever, a book based on Kim Il-sung's diary, is perhaps the most famous story that emerged from the "April 15th" group. It is said that Kim Jong-il put them up in a resort in Nampo, a port town on the western coast, in order for them to concentrate on the story. The writers finished the manuscript in a matter of weeks, which was one of the requirements. It is not known exactly how long it took, but Kim Byung-hoon and Baek In-joon are said to have developed an illness that required extensive medical attention when the work was completed.

The team of artists pressed on and produced the revolutionary masterpieces, such as *Commando Brothers Five, Fate of a Self-Defense Unit, Pibada (Sea of Blood), Flower Salesgirl, Talk to Me,* and *Milam.* Of these, *Pibada* and *Flower Salesgirl* were major contributions to the idolization of Kim Il-sung. *Pibada,* a story about a family's struggle against landowners and imperial Japan, impressed Kim Il-sung and his close comrades from his partisan days.

CHAPTER 3

KIM JONG-IL'S FIRST MARRIAGE

L ife for Kim Jong-il was not all work. It was about 1968 when he met a pretty actress named Sung Hye-rim, who had starred in an "April 15th" movie, *Fate of a Self-Defense Unit*. Five years older than Kim, she is said to have reminded him of his mother, initially attracting his attention. She had lived and gone to school in Seoul, South Korea, until following her parents to Pyongyang during the Korean War. She graduated from Pyongyang Film and Theater College in 1960.

Her father, Sung Yu-kyung, was an intellectual, as was her mother, and had joined the Communist Party in the South because of his association with Park Hun-young, the leader of the Southern Communist Party before the war. Her mother was a veteran reporter for Rodong Sinmun.

When Hye-rim went to Pyongyang Girls School Number 3, she became the chairperson for the student political organization. She was a beautiful sixteen-year-old, and "people stopped to take a second look at her when she walked by," according to her older sister Hye-rang. Upon her graduation from high school, Hye-rim went to the preparatory school for Kim Il-sung University but transferred to the art school, majoring in film and theater arts.

Her good looks and refined mannerism invited many proposals for marriage, including one from Lee Ki-young, the chairman of the

31

Chosun Writers Association. Hye-rim's parents agreed to Lee's marriage proposal, and Hye-rim, now nineteen years old, married Lee Pyung, Lee's oldest son.

Sung Hye-rim

It so happened that Lee's second son was a friend of Kim Jong-il, and Kim frequented their house riding his motorcycle. Sung Hye-rang recalls those days in her memoirs:

> The Premier's son, then in his teens attending Namsan High School, was no doubt fascinated by the sight of Hye-rim, an elegant new bride of incomparable beauty, wearing her long apron and greeting him with a shy smile, her eyes downcast. She was a picture that evoked the fragrance of his mother perhaps....

She continued her schooling at the film and theater arts school. In North Korea, married persons cannot go to college, but her mother persuaded the minister of cultural communications to make an exception for her. In 1959, she starred in a film entitled *A Village by the Divided Line,* which was a big hit. Kim Il-sung called the movie "a creative model for the traditional Chosun woman's character." She went on to become the principal actress of the Chosun Film Arts Studio, starring in a number of major movies.

It was only natural that Kim Jong-il, then the chief film producer for the Party Central, would run into Hye-rim once again. Once Kim began showing his interest in Hye-rim, she was accepted to the Party and given the title, "Distinguished Actress." She participated in international film festivals as well. Kim Jong-il began spending a lot of time with her, discussing screenplays, roles, and characters of ongoing or future films. He drove her to filming locations all over the countryside. He even took her in his helicopter to a shoot near BaikDu Mountain.

Lee Han-young, her nephew (Hye-rang's son), writes in his memoirs:[8]

> I happened to run across at home a trunk that was filled with my aunt's photographs. These pictures of my aunt with Kim Jong-il were taken at various resorts that I recognized as Kim Il-sung's retreats around the country. I knew then that she was dating him in secret. That was 1968, and they moved in together in 1969.
>
> This was significant enough for someone to report to Kim Il-sung, but no one had. Nor did anyone report about their son Jong-nam. He was born on May 10, 1971, and Kim Jong-il didn't tell his father about his secret marriage or Jong-nam until the boy was four years old.

Some experts suggest that Kim had forced himself on Hye-rim, then a married woman with a daughter. This doesn't seem likely, considering the fact that she and her husband, Lee Pyung, were already separated after a long, trying marriage that had begun when she was a nineteen-year-old going to the film school. She had a will of her own, pouring all her energy into acting and eventually rising to stardom. She was certainly not just a flower on the wall. She was a major celebrity, more recognizable than Kim Jong-il, and it was far riskier for her to be seen with him in public, for her image was that of a trophy wife for all North Korean men at the time. This explains their discreet affair in the countryside at isolated beaches and in the woods, known only to another couple who accompanied them on these outings. Countless

---

[8]   Lee Han-young, *Kim Jong-il Royal Family*, (Seoul: Shidae Jongshin, 2004). Lee Han-young defected to South Korea in 1982. He was assassinated in 1997.

photographs that Lee Han-young found in the trunk at his mother's home show nothing but a glorious romance and happy smiles.

So a genuine affection for each other makes more sense than unilateral conquest on Kim Jong-il's part. The romance culminated in their marriage, though in secret, followed by the birth of Jong-nam. The day Jong-nam was born, excited Kim Jong-il drove home from the hospital, honking his horn and yelling, "It's a boy, it's a boy." Hye-rang would remember that day as the happiest she'd ever seen him.

Life couldn't be better for them, living in a sprawling compound of their own, surrounded by luxury beyond comparison. Hye-rim was the queen, married to the heir apparent who would rule the country someday.

Kim Jong-il loved his son like no other. He provided a playroom for Jong-nam, about ten thousand square feet, and filled it with toys. His birthdays were a major event, preceded by a month-long search for birthday presents by embassy staff in Hong Kong, Tokyo, Geneva, Singapore, and Berlin. The presents poured into their palace through diplomatic pouches to the tune of about 1 million dollars. There was nothing Kim Jong-il wouldn't do for his little prince, who was said to be remarkably precocious. At times when Kim Jong-il ate dinner alone late at night, Jong-nam would keep his father company. Kim Jong-il would sit Jong-nam on the dinner table next to him while he ate. Jong-nam would peer at his father and ask, "Taste good, Papa?"

Once, Jong-nam had a loose tooth, and his dentist wanted to pull it out. He refused. His mother, Hye-rim, tried to talk to him, but he threw a fit, crying at the top of his lungs. So she called Kim Jong-il at his office. Kim Jong-il rushed over and tried to persuade Jong-nam, but to no avail. Kim Jong-il finally asked his son, "So, how can I get you to pull your tooth?" The boy paused and replied, "I want a car just like yours, Papa." Kim Jong-il agreed to buy him a Cadillac limousine, and the boy allowed the dentist to pull his tooth. Like a good father, Kim Jong-il kept his promise and bought his son the car, and Jong-nam rode in the Cadillac limousine with his bodyguards on his favorite outings: visiting various military bases around Pyongyang. The dream couple seemed to have everything they could hope for—a life of luxury, loving father, beautiful loving wife, and loving son.

They had a problem, though: they didn't know how to reveal Jong-nam's existence to Kim Il-sung, who was nagging Kim Jong-il to get married. "You're thirty-three years old already. You should get married and give me a grandson." They struggled with the question for a long time. Instead of telling his father that he had a grandson, he married Kim Young-sook, an attractive typist from his office, to appease his father. Kim Jong-il at this time was engaged in a ferocious battle against his uncle to become the successor, and he couldn't risk exposing Hye-rim and Jong-nam. That would surely jeopardize his chances.

Needless to say, Hye-rim was not happy about the fact that her husband had married another woman. Her troubles began when Kim Jong-il's sister, Kyoung-hui, got involved and voiced her solution to the problem. Known for her directness, Kyoung-hui told Hye-rim right out, "You are older than my brother, and you have been married. You have a daughter as well. I will raise Jong-nam. You should leave. I will make sure that you are well provided for."

Hye-rim replied, "Absolutely not. He is my son. I can't give him to you." And with that, she took Jong-nam and hid somewhere outside the compound, driving Kim Jong-il crazy. She eventually returned and told Kim Jong-il, "Jong-nam must be raised by his mother. I can't give him up. I'll take him to his grandfather myself."

Kim Jong-il asked her to hold off for a while. Months went by, and Hye-rim became worried that they would take her son away from her. Her health began to deteriorate. Their life of romance was doomed to fail. Their secluded life free of outside intervention was grand for a while, but the comfort of secrecy was a two-edged sword for them, especially for Hye-rim. Discretion was one thing, but she was living inside the compound surrounded by a twelve-foot fence with armed troops guarding both sides of the fence, and for a celebrity who was used to public adoration, she must have felt hemmed in. Hye-rim's condition worsened, both physically and mentally. She suffered a bad case of depression that required treatment. She received treatment first in Pyongyang and later in Moscow, sometimes for months at a time.

It wasn't until 1975 when Kim Jong-il informed his father of the secret marriage, well after Kim Jong-il was officially named as successor to the throne. Kim Il-sung was angry at first, but he relented when he learned about his grandson. It didn't take long for young Jong-nam to win over his grandfather.

Lee Han-young, Jong-nam's cousin writes in his memoirs, *Kim Jong-il's Royal Family*:

> Jong-nam ruled the roost, the king and the commander of the house. He was temperamental and stubborn as well. Once he became angry about something, no one could say anything to appease him. Everyone had to wait till he calmed down by himself.
>
> He liked guns a lot. Once, Kim Jong-il promised to get a Belgian pistol for the boy. The pistol didn't arrive on time, and Jong-nam threw a fit. He kept crying, refusing to eat. Kim Jong-il happened to mention to Kim Il-sung about Jong-nam's crying.
>
> He responded, "That's big trouble. I'll talk to the boy myself," as the story goes. Kim Il-sung, who happened to be meeting with a foreign dignitary at the time, turned to his visitor and said, "My grandson is crying and refusing to eat, upset about something. I'll go and calm him down. Let's meet after lunch."
>
> Kim Il-sung sent for Jong-nam and told him, "I'll keep my promise and punish the one who is late with the pistol." Only then the boy calmed down.

This episode shows us the extent of Kim Il-sung's affection for his grandson. The Great Leader who reigned over the fourth-largest army in the world, the omnipotent revolutionary with countless number of statues dedicated to him, including the famous sixty-five-foot bronze statue in the heart of Pyongyang, melted to nothing in the presence of the precocious boy with a penchant for guns. This boy, who had been born out of a secret marriage, rose out of hiding and onto center stage. This had to have been a tremendous relief for Kim Jong-il. He was now the official heir-apparent, no longer concerned about concealing the boy's existence. Had his political foes—his uncle, for instance—known about Jong-nam, they would have crucified him in front of the Party's Central Committee for his untoward activities, thus thwarting his bid for the job that he felt destined to succeed.

Kim Jong-nam (in the middle) at his father's
thirty-eighth birthday party

CHAPTER 4

KIM JONG-IL'S RISE TO POWER

H e was destined to follow his father to lead North Korea. His mother's last words to her partisan comrades were: "Please look after my son after I'm gone and help him become the leader just like his father."

His mother's dying words were prophetic, as it turned out. Her partisan comrades did look after her son and helped him become their leader, just as she had wished. However, the sharpshooting commando who once saved Kim Il-sung's life could not have foreseen all the troubles her son would have to go through to get there. Nor could she have imagined the catastrophe of the Korean War that began in 1950, the year after she died, that lasted for three years. Her partisan comrades stood by her husband and her family throughout the war and their struggles in the aftermath of the war.

Then came the 1960s and the *Chollima* era, when the country enjoyed relative peace and prosperity, followed by a period of internal strife with the Kapsan faction, who wanted to take the country in a different direction. Her partisan comrades stood by her husband, Kim Il-sung, again and helped him purge the Kapsan faction and restore order among the ranks. She never saw any of these events herself, but she had always believed her loyal comrades would support her husband.

It was also her comrades who helped the young Kim Jong-il into the Information Department of the Party, and he did not disappoint them. They loved the movies he made, depicting them as heroes. Catering to the partisan contingents was part of Kim Jong-il's plan, one he carefully laid out to win their support. He personally stayed in touch with all the members of the partisans and their children. He made sure they received the best gifts on holidays and at receptions he held for them. The partisan group loved Kim Jong-il.

Despite their support, however, it was paramount for him to gain his father's confidence if he was to replace his uncle as the successor. His uncle had been considered the designated successor for quite some time now, especially since the purge of the Kapsan faction in 1967. After all, Kim Young-ju, born in 1920, had been a partisan commando alongside his brother, Kim Il-sung. He later studied at Moscow University and returned to Pyongyang and became an advisor in the Workers' Party Organizational Department. The department oversaw the Party's personnel matters, among other responsibilities, which made it the most powerful department in the government. He was appointed as its head in 1960, and in 1966, he became the secretary of Political Committee of the Party, positioning himself as the number-two man next to Kim Il-sung. The Kapsan purge of March 1967 fortified Kim Il-sung's control over the Party and solidified Kim Young-ju's position. He came to enjoy his brother's complete trust, taking on secret missions such as negotiating the terms of unification with the government of South Korea, which culminated in the so-called "July 4 North-South Joint Communiqué" in 1972. Kim Young-ju represented North Korea in signing his name to the unprecedented agreement outlining a peaceful unification between the two Koreas. He also went to Egypt, Syria, Iraq, Romania, and Hungary as Kim Il-sung's special emissary, to strengthen ties with those countries. He seemed to have secured his position as the successor to Kim Il-sung.

That is, until Kim Jong-il came along. Undaunted by his uncle's solid résumé, Kim Jong-il, believing that he was the rightful successor, made his move against his uncle. He set out to prove that he was more devoted to Kim Il-sung than his uncle was. Kim Jong-il, then the deputy chief of the Information Department, focused all his energy and resources on idolizing his father as the supreme leader.

Not to be outdone by his young nephew, Kim Young-ju responded with his own plans to idolize his brother, as well as further developing the concept of "Kim Il-sung-ism," as a follow-up to Kim Il-sung's "May 25 Teaching." He sought to reinforce the concept of the monolithic system, anticipating that this would please Kim Il-sung. Thus, uncle and nephew became embroiled in a fierce battle of one-upmanship in idolizing and beatifying Kim Il-sung.

Book burning and cultural defoliation were well under way, and they rushed to fill the void with materials on Kim Il-sung. Phrases like "Kim Il-sung the Illuminator," "The Sun," "The Oracle," "The Omniscient," "The Divine," "Deity," and "The King of Light" appeared about this time. People in cities and countryside joined in the fray to express their words of worship. Kim Il-sung statues were erected, books on Kim Il-sung were printed, and movies idolizing Kim Il-sung were produced.

By a strange twist of fate, Kim Jong-il was appointed the deputy chief of Party Organizational Department directly under his uncle in September 1969. He had two deputy chief posts now, one at the Information Department and the other at the Party Organizational Department. As the deputy chief, he was in a position to control all the communications and personnel matters of the department, far more closely than its chief would. It didn't take long for him to take complete control of the department, especially when his uncle's health began deteriorating, which kept him away from his office. Moreover, the chief of the Information Department, Kim Guk-tae, had fallen ill, which gave Kim Jong-il a free hand running both departments without any interference whatsoever.

Kim Jong-il at work

He took advantage of his uncle's absence and promoted his loyal followers from the Party Organizational Department and the Information Department, Kye Ung-thae, Kang Song-san, Jon Byong-Ho, Han Sung-ryong, Seo Yoon-seok, and Choe Thae-bok, to name a few. Kim Jong-il brought on Choe Ik-gyu, his film tutor, to direct important public events such as Kim Il-sung's birthday celebrations. Kim Jong-il remembered to repay his supporters like Choi Hyon, the old partisan who had pushed for him at the Party political committee meetings. Choi Hyon's son, Choi Yong-hae, was appointed the chair of the Central Committee for the Kim Il-sung Socialist Youth Alliance, an important post in the Party Central.

Kim Jong-il also tapped heavily on his classmates from Kim Il-sung University to fill important positions in the Party. The majority of them were later assigned to the countryside, for fear that they knew too much about his background from his youth. He didn't want to risk any leakage of information on his private life. That is why Kim Jong-il proceeded to install "his" people in key positions as he overhauled the reporting structure. Like Kim Il-sung, he relied on his relatives and close friends, whom he felt he could trust.

Among the closest relatives were his sister, Kim Kyoung-hui, and her husband, Jang Song-thaek. They had met at Kim Il-sung University, where they were both students in the College of Economics. Kim Kyoung-hui liked Jang, a suave, smart man and an accomplished accordionist. When the word went around that she was dating Jang, her father, Kim Il-sung, ordered an investigation concerning his family background. He saw something he didn't like with respect to Jang's father and ordered Kyoung-hui to stop seeing Jang immediately. He also instructed his brother, Young-ju, to make sure that the two ended their relationship. Kim Young-ju went to see Hwang Jang-yop, then the president of the university, and asked for Hwang's help in keeping the two apart. Hwang didn't commit himself one way or the other, because he knew that any attempt to separate the two young people would backfire. He tried to see Jang a couple of times at his residence, though. Then Kyoung-hui paid Hwang a visit and complained, "Why are you, the president of the university, meddling in my love affair?"

Hwang relayed to Kim Young-ju what had happened with Kyoung-hui. Kim Young-ju shook his head and said, "She is so headstrong. Nobody can keep her under control."

Jang and Kyoung-hui continued to meet each other in secret, but it didn't take long for Kim Il-sung to find out. He ordered Jang to Wonsan University on the east coast. Kyoung-hui became sick, laid up in bed for weeks. Her stepmother, Kim Song-ae, saw that the situation was impossible and persuaded Kim Il-sung to back off. In the meantime, Kim Jong-il took time to study Jang up close, taking him around to movie studios and other facilities, and came to like him during the process. Eventually, Kim Jong-il recommended marriage for Jang and Kyoung-hui, and they got married after Jang graduated. Jang started to work for the Party's Organizational Department in Pyongyang, and so began his career inside the power circle. He moved on to direct the North Korean embassy network around the world and international trading, which included narcotics.

While he filled the important positions with the people he trusted, he began accusing his uncle of harboring Marxist ideas instead of the new Kim Il-sung-ism. Whenever he had a chance, he said, "Uncle's ideology is antiquated," or "Uncle's way of doing business belongs in the past." No doubt these accusations reached Kim Il-sung's ears.

Kim Jong-il's idolization campaign pushed ahead in earnest; he produced massive film projects and constructed monuments like the Arch of Triumph, which stands twenty meters (65.6 feet), the 558-foot JuChe Tower, a stadium with 150,000 seats, and Joson Museum of Revolution. He ordered the erection of Kim Il-sung statues in every province, county, and city. He built research institutes for Kim Il-sung, Kim Jong-sook (mother), and Kim Jong-il himself. Also, Kim Jong-il ordered the construction of the "tallest statue in the world" in the image of Kim Il-sung, which stands twenty meters high in Pyongyang. It was originally designed to stand twenty-seven meters tall, but the senior Kim objected as being "too ostentatious," and they reduced the height by seven meters. Also, the entire statue was gold-plated at first, which made the area around his eyes appear dark when the sunlight hit the statue. So they replaced it with bronze. Conceptually, Kim Jong-il's strategy for building his father's personality cult was simple: keep the people in the dark and feed them your brand of goods. He isolated all communication channels and kept feeding them heroic deeds that Kim Il-sung supposedly accomplished.

Hwang told me that Kim Il-sung was always humble about his own accomplishment as partisan freedom fighter against the Japanese imperialism, which agrees with Kim Il-sung's own account in his autobiography, *With the Century (Seh Ki-wa Deo Buruh)*. Somewhere along the way, however, Kim Il-sung became a conquering hero, as if he and his shabby, hungry band of commandos had demolished the mighty Japanese military machine all by themselves. He emerged bigger than life, made possible by Kim Jong-il and his blind ambition to succeed power.

It was at about this time that Kim Jong-il began building luxurious resorts and guesthouses all over the country for the Kims' exclusive use. Kim Jong-il was spending money like a madman, and a vice prime minister by the name of Kim Kyong-ryon brought up the issue at a Central Committee meeting and said, "Resorts, statues, and special construction projects cost too much. Let's put this money into the economy."

Sometime after this meeting, Kim Kyong-ryon was not seen in public again. No one spoke up against the idolization projects ever again.

The idolization campaign forged ahead, and according to North Korean diplomats who served in African countries, there was even a campaign to create a cult following overseas. In 1974, they built a North Korean-style division in Zaire's army, providing it with all the necessary material, to the tune of 150 million US dollars. In addition to Zaire, Kim Jong-il provided generous support to Tanzania, Zambia, Algeria, Madagascar, Burundi, Rwanda, Mali, Burkina Faso, and Guinea, all for Kim Il-sung's glory. In 1987, North Korea built the Kim Il-sung Stadium in Tanzania, which cost about 50 million US dollars. They built offices for the presidents of Madagascar and Togo, and a parliament building for the Central African Republic.

Then Kim Jong-il initiated the biggest coup of them all. What followed was *Kim Il-sung's Ten Principles,* which completely changed the way of life in North Korea like never before. Originally, *Kim Il-sung's Ten Principles* was Kim Young-ju's idea for reinforcing Kim Il-sung's "monolithic system," but Kim Jong-il was the one to give it water and let it take its roots. Kim Jong-il reworked its wording and distributed it throughout the country, along with an instruction for people to memorize Kim Il-sung's new doctrine.

By this time, his uncle was completely out of picture. Kim Jong-il turned on his propaganda machine full blast and pushed the new monolithic ethos—no doubt pleasing his father to no end. Kim Young-ju would disappear from the scene, never to be seen in public for the following eighteen years starting in 1975. It was the implementation of the Ten Principles that catapulted Kim Jong-il to the forefront.

Ultimately, Kim Jong-il credits his mother for his rise to power. His devotion to his departed mother—who had died when he was eight years old—would remain strong throughout his life. There is a famous episode involving a foreign minister of the African Guinea who was in Pyongyang for medical treatment in September 1987. Two days after his arrival, he visited Kim Il-sung at his office. The diplomat commented, "I have read that your first wife, Kim Jong-sook, was a great woman. I would like to express my admiration for Madam Kim Jong-sook who has devoted her life to you with undying loyalty."

There was no way the diplomat could have known about Kim Jong-sook. As it turned out, the North Korean ambassador had briefed him and pleaded with him to say something about her. When Kim Jong-il heard the report about the diplomat's comment about his mother, he ordered Kang Sok-ju (then first deputy foreign minister) to treat the African diplomat as a state guest, praising the foreign minister from Guinea for his insight about his mother. "How could he have known about Comrade Kim Jong-sook and that she was a great person? This is a wonderful development. Our foreign ministry seems to be doing a good job over there." Immediately, the diplomat's lodging was upgraded from the Koryo Hotel to the VIP residence as a state guest, and his limousine upgraded to a Benz 380. He also received medical treatment at the hospital dedicated for the exclusive use of Kim Il-sung and Kim Jong-il.

After the medical treatment, Kim Jong-il extended a special invitation to the diplomat to spend an unscheduled vacation at the VIP resort in the Myo Hyang Mountains. The diplomat went out to the Pyongyang railroad station that evening. He was surprised to find that the station was empty but for a protocol officer from the North Korean Foreign Ministry. The official explained, "This train is called the Train Number 1, which means that the train is for the premier's use only. Comrade Kim Jong-il made it available for you."

The diplomat was astonished at the train car, which was equipped with a bedroom, library, reception room, and office. He was able to travel in luxury all because of his innocent praise for Madam Kim Jong-sook.

Kim Jong-il's affection for his mother and related stories are legendary. He fell in love with his first wife, actress Sung Hye-rim, because she reminded him of his mother. Years later, he was asked by a Russian reporter, "Who would you say is the closest person to you?"

He replied, "My mother, may she rest in peace. My mother would never have imagined the way I turned out. I owe her a great deal."

A NEW WORLD: KIM IL-SUNG'S TEN PRINCIPLES

According to Hwang, familiarity with Kim Il-sung's Ten Principles is the key to understanding North Korean society. Without it, nothing makes sense. Young and old, everyone has to memorize and recite the principles at Party meetings, schools, farms, factories, and offices across the country. This practice has gone on for the past forty years, and this doctrine supersedes any other form of rules or laws, such as North Korea's Socialist Constitution or the JuChe Philosophy. Here is my translation of the Ten Principles:

Principle 1

For our Great Leader Kim Il-sung and his revolutionary ideals, we must fight with our lives to unitize all of our society. Transforming our society into a singular entity in accordance with our Su Ryong's revolutionary ideals is our Party's ultimate command, a new step toward building a monothematic governing structure.

Principle 2

For our Great Leader Kim Il-sung, we must pledge and dedicate our loyalty to him. Devoting our endless loyalty to our Su Ryong is our most sublime duty as a revolutionary. It is the way to everlasting glory for our fatherland and our people's happiness forever.

Principle 3

For our Great Leader Kim Il-sung, we must bestow upon him absolute authority. It is prerequisite for our revolution and the revolutionary will of our Party and the people.

Principle 4

For our Great Leader Kim Il-sung, we must accept and believe in his revolutionary ideals and adopt them as our creed. This is the most important requirement in becoming JuChe communist revolutionaries with the utmost loyalty to Su Ryong; it is a predestined condition for our revolutionary struggles and for the successful construction of our society.

Principle 5

For our Great Leader Kim Il-sung, we must absolutely abide by the original principles of his teachings in executing them. Carrying out his teachings without any precondition is the fundamental requirement for our loyalty to our Su Ryong; it is crucial in our revolutionary struggles and for the successful construction of our society.

Principle 6

We must rally around our Great Leader Kim Il-sung and intensify our effort in unifying the Party's ideological intent and consolidating our revolutionary goals. Our unity, as strong as steel, is the power base for the Party's victory and the resolute foundation for our victorious revolution.

Principle 7

We must learn from our Great Leader Kim Il-sung and acquire his communist ways, his revolutionary methods in industrial and social endeavors. To learn from him is the sacred duty of all Party members and workers and a prerequisite for fulfilling the glorious tasks as the Su Ryong's revolutionary soldier.

Principle 8

Our Great Leader Kim Il-sung has bequeathed us political will and our life. We must guard it with care and reciprocate his great gift with our loyalty that reflects our own political cognizance and skills of high order. It is our infinite glory that our Great Leader Kim Il-sung is the source of our political will and life. In reciprocating our Su Ryong's political trust with our loyalty, we must deem the political will and our life with the highest priority among all forms of life. We must never compromise our political belief and revolutionary principles, even to the final moment of our life.

Principle 9

We must firmly establish order for the Party, State, and Military so that they can consistently function as a single unit under the leadership of our Great Leader Kim Il-sung. Establishing the sole, unique leadership structure of our Great Leader Kim Il-sung is a basic requirement in strengthening the Party structure ideologically and for enhancing the Party's capability in its leadership role, as well as a guarantee for the victory in our revolution and construction of the State.

Principle 10

We must inherit the revolutionary work pioneered by our Great Leader Kim Il-sung and continue his work to its completion. Establishing the singular leadership structure advances our Great Su Ryong's revolution in perpetuity and guarantees our ultimate victory.

What do these principles mean? Here are some examples about the Ten Principles to help us understand the specifics that these words represent. For instance, the third principle says, "For our Great Leader Kim Il-sung—we must bestow upon him absolute authority. It is prerequisite for our revolution and the revolutionary will of our Party and the people." Article 6 of the Third Principle further states, "Su Ryong Comrade Kim Il-sung's portraits, busts, statues, badges containing his portrait, publications containing his portrait, art paintings containing his portrait, signs displaying his teachings, and the Party's basic motto must be treated with reverence and protected with utmost care."

Portraits of Kim Il-sung and Kim Jong-il hang in every living room in North Korea. These pictures have to be carefully dusted every day with a clean cloth, never with a household rag. A dusty portrait spells trouble for the family, including incarceration as political prisoners. A cavalier treatment of their images is a serious offense and is treated as deconsecrating. A newspaper containing either of their pictures is not a mere newspaper; it is a piece of Holy Scripture. Sitting or stepping on it is a blasphemous act, deserving severe punishment.

These rules have become ritualized, and North Korean people in general believe and practice them with genuine zeal. Some years back, there was an interesting incident at an international athletic event held in South Korea. North Korea was a participant, and a good number of athletes and staff were housed at an Olympic village, where a placard with Kim Jong-il's photo and his message hung nearby. Everything was fine until the day it rained. North Korean personnel swarmed in front of the placard in tears, shocked that the event officials had left the placard with Kim's photo in the rain. They carefully took it down, sobbing as they did so. Their tearful outrage was sensationalized by the news, and the people of the South thought this behavior was rather odd.

Odd behavior or not, their outburst appeared genuine, not a manufactured show for the Party politicos back in Pyongyang, as some South Korean press reports suggested.

Nobody knew where their true motivation came from, but their behavior was consistent with Article 6 of the Third Principle.

The rules are very specific about the Party members as well. All the Party members belong to a cell comprised of five to thirty members under the direction of the cell secretary. Article 5 of the Eighth Principle requires that all the members undergo a process called "life integration," similar to public confession/self-criticism.

> Every two days, the Party members must participate in "life integration," examine, integrate their lives and work in accordance with high ideological standards. All members must develop their ideological struggle through this critical method, and through this ideological struggle, members must train themselves in revolutionary ideals and ceaselessly rebuild themselves.

One begins his or her life integration session with the recital of the appropriate principles, Kim Il-sung's teachings, or Kim Jong-il's directives, whichever may be related to the particular self-examination session. This process is similar to the reading of certain phrases out of the Bible prior to a discussion. Then the member describes his or her mistakes in front of the members and offers self-criticism. Theoretically speaking, Kim Il-sung and Kim Jong-il, as members of the Workers' Party, are required to attend "life integration" sessions, but they are not known to have participated in any.

The cell secretary is required to file a report to the Party Commission at the end of each day of all the events that had occurred during the day, positive or negative. These reports must be complete and thorough, for anything less would violate Article 8 of the Ninth Principle, triggering a grueling interrogation.

This is how Kim Jong-il stayed on top of the Party members—by maintaining tight cell structure—and Hwang Jang-yop was all too familiar with Kim's dragnet. Hwang saw Kim Jong-il up close and watched him keep Party personnel in check by handing down punishments ranging from warnings to exiles. Even top officials like Jang Song-thaek, his brother-in-law, and Kim Yong-soon, a party elite, endured re-education through forced labor for violating some or all of the following rules:

One must possess a clear and definite attitude that Great Leader Kim Il-sung is all-knowing, the only one who knows anything.

Third Principle, Article 3

With regard to an official's directive, recipients of the directive must confirm that the directive conforms to the thoughts and policies of the Great Leader. If one detects any deviance, he must immediately challenge the directive and question it. One must not quote an individual official and pass it on or discuss it as a "decision" or a "directive" of the Party.

Fourth Principle, Article 8

An individual official is not permitted to organize lower level meetings at his whim, be it a Party, government office, or labor organization. Nor is he permitted to behave so unorganized a manner as to hand down a decision arbitrarily.

Ninth Principle, Article 5

One must vigorously challenge and fight any individual official who goes beyond the limits of his authority or abuses his power.

Ninth Principle, Article 6

No one was immune to these principles, as Kim Jong-il ruthlessly applied them to root out his opponents. While most of the original partisans supported his designation as the heir apparent, he faced opposition from various individuals who regarded the "monarchist" succession of power as improper. Chief among them was Kim Tong-kyu, the former partisan commando under Kim Il-sung, as well as Nam Il, then the vice prime minister. They expressed dissatisfaction even after the official announcement in February 1974. Nam Il was found dead, crushed by a truck in a Pyongyang alley in March 1976, an event that warranted only a brief mention in the daily *Rodong Sinmun* (newspaper).

In June 1976, Kim Tong-kyu openly criticized Kim Jong-il at a Political Committee meeting. He said, "Kim Jong-il is giving the families of partisans special treatment and together they are breaking the Party rules and procedures ... we're rushing too much to install Kim

Jong-il as the successor … we should proceed slowly, so as to give people a chance to digest the concept … Kim Jong-il is showing disrespect for the older Party officials."

Kim Tong-kyu was a force to reckon with, triggering a fierce debate among the Party cadre. In the end, however, Kim Tong-kyu sealed his own fate by challenging Kim Jong-il. By the end of 1977, he was incarcerated for violating Kim Il-sung's Ten Principles and was moved to a political prison in South Ham Kyung Province along with his close colleagues. During the process, about three hundred thousand Party members suspected of any connection with Kim Tong-kyu lost their membership, and they were replaced by six hundred thousand younger Party members.

Anyone who violates the Ten Principles is promptly punished. Hwang said, "When an official loses his position or gets kicked out of the Party, he gets assigned to a farm or a mine. Immediately, he loses his house, his car, telephone, and all the privileges that come with the position. He and his family lose medical privileges, and his children lose college admission privileges. This is the reason why the Party officials never complain."

When Hwang first arrived in South Korea, he was surprised that the South Korean scholars were unaware of *Kim Il-sung's Ten Principles:*

> "When I came to the South, I found more books about the North than I had expected. I saw volumes of books related to Kim Il-sung, books on JuChe philosophy, and frankly, I was surprised, especially when you consider the fact that an average person in the North cannot possess a single book related to the South.
>
> Anyone found with any material about South Korea would be arrested. Books related to the South cannot even exist in the library. So I thought that the quality of research on North Korea was good. When I gave speeches on North Korea, I found that the general public readily accepted my views.
>
> However, I have problems with the so-called experts on North Korea. They don't believe what I say. It's not just me. Other defectors are puzzled why the scholars do not believe what they say about North Korea. Some scholars seem to think that they know more about North Korea than I do, and I am appalled at this.

At first, I thought that it was possible that they actually did know more than I did because they were the experts. But as time went on, I learned that was false. I realized that these scholars, not all of them of course, had no inkling of what Kim Jong-il's regime really was.

Kim Il-sung's Ten Principles is a prime example. I repeatedly tell them that *Kim Il-sung's Ten Principles* are the governing rules and that they precede the Socialist Constitution or the Workers' Party regulations, but they don't believe me.

All these years, the North Korean studies curriculum in the South has been based on a false premise. I don't know how they claim to be the experts on North Korea without a clear understanding of *Kim Il-sung's Ten Principles*. It seems to me that they don't know anything about the true Kim Jong-il."

CHAPTER 5

KIM JONG-IL TAKES CONTROL

—————⟶≫●≪⟵—————

ECONOMY

F inancing idolization projects costs a great deal of money, and Kim
Jong-il needed a free hand in financing them. He devised a method
to segregate the economic resources into three tiers: Party economy,
military economy, and national economy. There was no one around
to oppose him, not even his uncle, who was completely out of the
picture by now. Hwang was convinced that Kim Jong-il's brainchild
on economics was the cause of the overall economic downfall of North
Korea. Hwang told me:

> "After he came to power in the 1970s, Kim Jong-il's priority
> was to differentiate Party finances from national economics.
> He established a separate economic unit for the Party in
> the name of managing the Party businesses which included
> covert revolutionary activities such as the liberation of
> South Korea and international communist party activities.
> In establishing a separate economic unit for the Party, Kim
> Jong-il selected well-equipped business entities, especially
> those with significant earning records in foreign currency,
> and grouped them together. In other words, he took the
> cream of the crop and set up an independent economic unit
> [under his control].

Gold mines were the first to become enlisted into the Party economy because gold could be converted into foreign currency. As time went on, all the factories and business entities of any importance were included in the Party's economics unit.

The Party's own [conglomerate] unit grew, and so did the Party's financial management bureau, dubbed as "Room 39" and "Room 38," which Kim controlled personally. Many business entities came under the auspice of Rooms 38 and 39 and received special treatment as the Party's exclusive companies.

[North Korea's] lack of electric power is a well-known fact. These companies under the direct control of the Party have priority in receiving electricity. The Party has the monopoly on expensive export products such as *shiitake* mushrooms, abalone, and other native products. Also, [Rooms 38 and 39] oversee drug trade and counterfeit operations."

Thus, Kim Jong-il built the Party conglomerate to finance his private projects, especially those intended for the idolization of Kim Il-sung. These projects included underground facilities for Kim Il-sung and Kim Jong-il, bodyguards numbering over one hundred thousand, and exclusive resorts, all at an enormous cost. Hwang believed that these monies would have been better spent on reinvesting in productive endeavors on behalf of the national economy. Instead, Kim Jong-il effectively cut the money circulation by half. This proved Kim Jong-il's lack of knowledge in the field of economics, as far as Hwang was concerned, despite the fact that Kim had majored in economics at Kim Il-sung University. Hwang recalled, "One day I talked to Kim Jong-il's professor. He told me that Kim Jong-il had little patience and stayed away from anything complicated."

Kim was interested in attaining power rather than contemplating economic policies or the future of the country. He needed to secure his father's trust and simply focused on projects that yielded immediate results. Hwang wrote: [9]

---

[9] Hwang Jang-yop, *Sunshine Siding with Darkness Cannot Illuminate: Hwang Jang-yop's Exposure of Secrets,* Korean, Hwang Jang-yop Birok Gong Gae: Uh Doom-ui Pyeon-i-doen Hatbyeot-un Uh Doom-eul Balkil-su-uhp-dah, (Seoul: Chosun Monthly, 2001).

Kim Jong-il ignored financial concerns as he drove hard for the completion of his projects, wasting tremendous financial resources and manpower. He ignored fundamental economic principles and invited national economic disaster.

For instance, in coal production, he set an impossible production target and demanded compliance. The miners, hard-pressed to meet the quota, nearly depleted the existing coal reserve, while neglecting to explore for new reserves.

Kim Jong-il rewarded those who met the quota regardless of what happened to the coal reserve. As a result, the coal-mining industry came dangerously close to shutting down.

Nonetheless, Kim Jong-il gave Kim Il-sung glowing reports. As the Party gained total control of the country's major industries, the Party politicos, not the economic experts, were left in charge of the nation's economy, making a huge mess [of North Korea's economy].

North Korea's economy took a nosedive in 1985, according to Hwang, who was in charge of the "Document Compilation Center," where he saw all the economic reports come through. He said, "All the data showed negative economic growth from 1985 on." Kim Jong-il, however, continued to send up false reports to Kim Il-sung.

He pushed for megaprojects, calling for transformation of Pyongyang as "the world's foremost modern city," ordering construction of massive athletic facilities in competition with the 1988 Olympics held in South Korea.

FOREIGN RELATIONS

With Kim Jong-il in control of the Party, the reporting structure changed in terms of foreign relations as well. He instructed officials at the foreign desk to report to both him and Kim Il-sung simultaneously on matters of international affairs. Up to that point, officials were reporting directly to Kim Il-sung, comfortable in thinking that Kim Il-sung represented the nation on the international stage. Kim Jong-il changed that. A former diplomat made this observation:[10]

> In November 1980, Ri Jong-mok (First Department Chair, Foreign Affairs) received a call from Kim Jong-il. Kim's crackling sound pierced Ri's ear. "The Foreign Affairs Department has no rules. Too often, you report important matters directly to Geum Su San [colloquial code for Kim Il-sung's office] and you don't bother to report to me. You should run the department like the military and set up your reporting structure like the military unit, so it can move more quickly, more thoroughly."
>
> There was a direct telephone line between Kim Jong-il's office and the Minister of Foreign Affairs and its First Department. This telephone had a small tape recorder. Sound technicians in the First Department edited the tape to beautify the spoken words by Kim Il-sung and Kim Jong-il. In particular, Kim Jong-il speaks very fast and he is very difficult to understand unless you completely focus. Ri embarked on reforming the departmental structure after his conversation with Kim Jong-il.
>
> There was a state visit by an African presidential delegation in the spring of 1985. The Foreign Affairs Ministry was busy preparing a report for Kim Jong-il, when the telephone rang. The call was from a staff member in Kim Il-sung's office.
>
> "I am Han Sung-bok from the Su Ryong's office. The visiting president arrived at the VIP guesthouse ten minutes ago. Why haven't you reported this to Su Ryong yet? How many lives do you think you have?" The lowly staffer from

---

[10] K.J. Sohn, *Kim Jong-il Report,* (Seoul: Bada Publishing, 2003), p. 149, excerpt translated by John Cha

Kim Jong-il's office snapped back, "Why are you talking to me that way?" and hung up on Han.

Then he called his boss and complained, "I can't go on like this, comrade Chief. I haven't had time to report to comrade Dear Leader Kim Jong-il yet, and Su Ryong's office is threatening to chop off my neck for not reporting to Su Ryong's office first."

"Who is talking garbage like that?"

"Han Sung-bok."

"I see. I'll straighten it all out for good this time," his boss declared and called his boss, Kim Jong-il.

Kim Jong-il immediately replied, "From now on, all matters regarding foreign affairs come to me first. Don't report to Geum Su San first. I'll take care of the rest."

That evening, the lowly staff member from Kim Jong-il's office received a call from Han Sung-bok. Han apologized, "I'm sorry for the telephone call earlier this afternoon. It was my mistake. I am ashamed that I behaved that way toward the Party (Kim Jong-il). Please keep us informed of what you report to the Party Political Bureau." Han was completely humble.

This is not to say that Kim Jong-il exercised sole control over foreign affairs. He always consulted his father before he acted, because he couldn't deny the fact that Kim Il-sung represented the country. There's another significant episode regarding the change in the reporting structure.[11]

In November of 1987, North Korea received an invitation to attend an event in Moscow in commemoration of the 70th anniversary of the October revolution. Representing North Korea were Park Sung-chul and Kim Young-nam. The team formulated their plan of activities for their visit to Moscow, one of which was to present an invitation to Mikhail Gorbachev for a visit to Pyongyang.

Kim Jong-il saw the plan and lost his temper. He called Kim Young-nam and said, "Don't invite Gorbachev." Kim Jong-il hated Gorbachev because of his *glasnost* (openness)

---

[11] Ibid., p.151, excerpt translated by John Cha

and *perestroika* (restructure) policy, characterizing him as a revisionist worse than Khrushchev.

Then, several days later, Kim Il-sung called Kim Young-nam and asked, "How's the preparation going for the Moscow visit?"

"Everything is going well, Su Ryong-nim."

"Good. When you get to Moscow, make sure to invite Gorbachev. Of course, I don't think he will visit us, but there is a saying that you always give more cake to the one you dislike, isn't there? Do your best."

"Yes, sir. I'll be sure to remember."

Kim Young-nam was in a difficult situation. He called a meeting with the top officials in the Foreign Affairs. They decided to report the situation to Kim Jong-il again. Kang Sok-ju sent a fax to Kim Jong-il, informing of Kim Il-sung's instructions and waited. The answer came on the eve of their departure to Moscow. "Go ahead and do what the Su Ryong-nim said."

They invited Gorbachev to come to Pyongyang, but he didn't accept the invitation. The conflicting orders from the father and the son often put the officials in a difficult spot. For example, there was a difference of opinion about a co-educational system. Kim Il-sung harbored Confucian values in terms of family structure and gender relations. He thought that boys and girls should not be in school together. He prohibited dating or marriage among college students. If a female college student happened to become pregnant while in school, she was expelled. If students got married while they were studying abroad, such as in Moscow, he required that one of the couple return home. Kim Hyong-jik, former professor in the Teachers College, recalls the following incident.[12]

> Kim Il-sung had a policy of separating the boys and girls at school, and he prohibited marriage until college graduation. It was late in the 1970s when many students who studied in the Soviet Union and Eastern Europe came back and became Party officials. They had the opinion that a co-educational system was better and sent up a suggestion to Kim Il-sung.

---

[12] Ibid., pp.152-153, excerpt translated by John Cha

Kim Il-sung was outraged. He said, "Whose idea was this! They're all revisionists! Fire them and re-educate them!"

Subsequently, several members of Science Education Department and Education Committee of the Party Political Bureau were terminated and sent to re-indoctrination.

Ten years later, Kim Jong-il said in a meeting, "Men and women do better in a mixed environment. That's human nature. Re-examine the segregated system and fix it." Kim Jong-il instructed the education committee to start with elementary schools.

The committee members were in a quandary. If Kim Il-sung found out, that would mean the end of life for them. They discussed this problem with all the concerned parties, but no answer came.

Then someone had a brilliant idea. Seeing as that Kim Il-sung was no longer engaged in on-site supervision, there was no way for him to find out if they changed to a co-educational system.

This idea worked to the end. By that time, all the reporting went through Kim Jong-il, and there was no way for Kim Il-sung to find out about the change.

Thus, a co-educational system was instituted in elementary schools throughout North Korea toward the end of the 1980s. Fortunately for the committee, Kim Il-sung didn't go on outings for on-site supervision sessions other than touring factories and farms.

These examples show how Kim Jong-il took over the reins, and by 1987, there was no doubt that Kim Jong-il was completely in charge. Kim Jong-il stopped sending written reports to Kim Il-sung, other than a few special occasions, citing his father's failing eyes. Instead, he had them record the reports so that his father could listen to the taped report in comfort, which effectively lessened the number of reports and took Kim Il-sung away from decision-making.

A former North Korean diplomat recollected an incident in the Ministry of Foreign Affairs:[13]

In January 1987, Kim Jong-il telephoned Kim Young-nam, then Minister of Foreign Affairs, and told him, "Su Ryong-

---

[13] Ibid., pp.153-155, excerpt translated by John Cha

nim's [Kim Il-sung] seventy-fifth birthday is approaching. This time, I would like to have leaders from twenty countries join us in the celebration."

This directive turned the ministry upside down; there weren't enough countries with whom we had relations. We held meetings for two weeks, but all we could come up with were six leaders from Africa and four from Eastern Europe. Ultimately, we made plans to invite ten heads of state.

We wrote a long proposal to Kim Jong-il, "... According to your directive, we vigorously pursued to invite twenty heads of state for the Su Ryong-nim's birthday celebration. As a result of our study in cooperation with our embassies around the world, we concluded that there are ten countries that could respond to our invitation. However, the ministry will do its utmost to invite twenty heads of state ..."

We sent up the proposal and waited with abated breath. At 10 AM on a Saturday toward the end of January, the intercom came on and announced: "All those who are involved in the invitation, report to the Minister's office immediately."

We hurried up to the Minister's office and found Kim Young-nam and Kang Sok-ju, their faces, grave and ashen. Kim Young-nam finally spoke in a tense voice, "We failed our Dear Leader in a big way. Everyone, including myself, shall take out their Party membership card and put them on the table."

Now, parting with the Party card is a serious matter. It means the end of one's political life, and everyone pulled out their Party card and put it on the table, their hands trembling. Kim Young-nam spoke again, "All right, then. This is the proposal that we had sent up. Take a good look at it and you can see why we don't deserve to be a Party member."

We looked at our written proposal after it came back from Kim Jong-il. It didn't have Kim Jong-il's signature or the date, as it usually did when he reviewed proposals. This one simply had a large, heavy "X" scribed on the face of the cover page. I could tell that Kim Jong-il stroked his pen in anger. His pen had gone through the paper.

Kim Young-nam spoke as he flipped the torn cover, "Dear Leader said, 'If I ask for twenty, you should invite twenty. Inviting ten is a disobedient attitude toward the Party.' Comrade Kang Sok-ju and I will prepare a letter of self-examination for our Dear Leader and a proposal for us to go to re-indoctrination. Now, get out, all of you. I can't stand the sight of you."

We all thought that this was the end. We were headed for a mine, or a farm. A factory, at best.

One day after the proposal of self-examination went up, Kim Jong-il sent his reply: "You shall invite twenty heads of state per my instruction." We were saved. We took back our Party card and went to work on the invitations. That was early February. We sent out special task force to all six continents for the celebration on April 15. Come April 15, five heads of state came to Pyongyang for the birthday celebration.

Reports to Kim Jong-il were called *proposal documents,* and they helped him keep his finger in all the departmental affairs. If he liked a particular proposal, he wrote, "Well done," "Totally agree," or "Agree" on the cover and signed his name and dated it. If his name and date appeared on the document, it immediately became law. If the proposal didn't attract his attention, he merely wrote down the date, signifying for reference that he had read it. If the report came back with only a date written on it, the department turned upside down with harsh charges of wasting the Dear Leader's valuable time by sending up a useless proposal.

In the early 1980s, the First Department of the Ministry of Foreign Affairs sent up a simple briefing on "Black Cat, White Cat," an economic policy formulated by Deng Hsiao Peng, the Chinese premier. With this famous phrase, Deng had settled the fierce argument regarding China's direction on economy, between the socialist planned economy and capitalist market economy. "Black or white, the color of the cat doesn't matter as long as it hunts mice well." Deng's brilliant statement paved the way for China's reform toward a market economy.

In sending him a briefing on Deng's policy, officials in the First Department thought Kim Jong-il should know about it. But they angered him instead. Kim Jong-il called Kim Young-nam and said, "Deng's black-cat-and-white-cat theory clearly is about opportunism and revisionism. Those Chinamen have abandoned socialist principles and are behaving like bunch of dogs. But we must stay on our course. We have relations with China, so don't openly criticize your men, but warn them very clearly of our position."

Kim Young-nam relayed Kim Jong-il's verbal instruction to his men. Despite the verbal warning, however, the men at the China desk made the judgment that the new developments were important, especially in light of the fact that China had established relations with South Korea, causing a major headache for the North Korean diplomatic corps. A former Foreign Affairs official explains what happened next: [14]

> In October 1988, the China desk of the First Department filed a follow-up report entitled, "China's Open-Market Policy and Its Result" for Kim Jong-il.
>
> The report contained detailed information on Deng's pursuit of open-market policy and its background, its effects, its impact on North Korea, and its pros and cons.
>
> The report came back with a scribble on the front cover, "Who asked to produce this kind of rubbish report on the Chinese open-market policy?"
>
> This meant trouble: Kim Jong-il was very angry. A "Great Discussion" session ensued in the Ministry's auditorium with all of the personnel in attendance. A "Great Discussion" is a grueling session involving the interrogation and criticism of the responsible person with respect to his ideology. The session can go on for months. This time, the Chief of the First Department took the stand, with Ri Hwa-sun (Vice Chief, Party Organizational Department) conducting the meeting. Ri charged the Chief of the First Department as a "reformist and a revisionist who was unduly attempting to introduce Chinese-style reform."
>
> The Chief, nearly half-dead at the end of the session, finally relented and offered a self-criticism, "I repaid our Dear Leader's grace with ingratitude."
>
> At the end of the ordeal, he was spared of harsh punishment. He was demoted.

These examples show the extent Kim Jong-il went to attain his control over the Ministry of Foreign Affairs. He circumvented his father's authority as head of state by sending up selected reports, thereby rendering his father ineffective and misinformed in foreign affairs. He was the de facto head of state now.

---

[14] Ibid., p.156, excerpt translated by John Cha

THE MILITARY

Kim Jong-il's next conquest was the military, the second most important element in securing his power. He was always mindful of the opposition among the hierarchy or a conspiracy to change his status as the designated successor. For this reason, he rushed to establish a monolithic governing system centered on Kim Il-sung-ism and kept everyone else away from the power circle. (The tenth principle of *Kim Il-sung's Ten Principles*.)

Support from the military provided concrete proof that he was indeed the heir apparent, and he used all the tools available to him to establish his presence among the ranks. In North Korea, the Party comes before the military. Since the 1970s, when he became the chief of the Party's Organizational Department, it had been within his purview to keep contact or meddle with the military personnel structure. This is significant because the military's political officers receive their instructions from the Organizational Department. Moreover, the department has tremendous influence on promotions and assignments, as well as the power to inspect and review military matters.

As the chief of the Organizational Department, Kim Jong-il instituted a new "information network" and placed information officers on all military bases larger than a regiment. These informers reported directly to the Party headquarters on the lives of military commanders, Party officers, and security officers, bypassing lower-level political officers. Important reports concerning the upper echelon went directly to the chief of the Organizational Department, Kim Jong-il. Reports consisted of straight facts such as "So-and-so did what, where, and when," with no interpretation or point of view.

Thus, Kim Jong-il was able to keep on top of military matters. In reality, however, a general by the name of O Jin-U ran the military at the same time Kim Jong-il was vying for its complete control. He had served under Kim Il-sung as a commando during the partisan days and rose up the ranks to become minister of the People's Armed Forces in 1976. A true confidant of Kim Il-sung, O was said to be the only person who could smoke cigarettes in his presence. They were that close, and O didn't report to anyone else.

Kim Jong-il needed O on his side. The problem was that O had sided with Kim Il-sung's second wife (Kim Song-ae) and her brother (Kim Song-gap) on several issues in the past. These issues dealt with Kim Jong-il's battle to clear away his would-be competitors to power, i.e., his uncle, his stepmother, and his stepbrothers, the "minor branches" that cluttered the Kim family tree. The "pure branches" of the Kim family tree heralded from Kim Jong-sook, true mother of the fatherland, true independence fighter, and true revolutionary. Therefore, he argued that he carried the true revolutionary blood in him.

O didn't like Kim Jong-il's information network within the military because he felt Kim Jong-il was undermining his authority. One day, he accidentally discovered that his office was bugged. He first suspected that his assistant was directed by Kim Jong-il to plant the bug and sacked him. He eventually found out from one of his intelligence officers that Pak Jong-guk, his newly appointed deputy director, was the culprit. He also found out that Pak was a drinking buddy of Jang Song-thaek, Kim Jong-il's brother-in-law. O went to see Kim Il-sung straight away and said, "Su Ryong-nim, I can't go on with my duties. Someone bugged my office. Am I a traitor? Am I a Southern spy? I, O Jin-U, want to resign from the ministry, sir."

Kim Il-sung was shocked. "Is this true?"

"Have you ever seen me lie to you? Pak Jong-guk, my new deputy, seems to be responsible."

"Pak Jong-guk?"

"Yes. I already knew that he was cocky and had no respect. It is up to you, Su Ryong-nim, but please get rid of him or let me go."

Pak Jong-guk promptly lost his military status. What is interesting is that Pak was then made ambassador to Cuba. It is a great honor to be assigned to North Korea's close ally, and it was only possible because of Kim Jong-il. The incident is an example of the acrid relationship between Kim Jong-il and O Jin-U over the years. Starting in 1980, Kim Jong-il initiated a different tack, presenting O with expensive gifts, six cars, and a new luxury house. O's view of Kim Jong-il softened somewhat when Kim Jong-il became an executive committee member of the Political Bureau, which consisted of Kim Il-sung, Kim Il, O Jin-U, Kim Jong-il, and Ri Jong-ok as of the Sixth Party assembly in October 1980. However, they kept their distance.

Their relationship took a dramatic turn in 1987, when O was involved in a near-fatal automobile accident. A motorcycle patrolman was passing by the War Victory Memorial Hall at three in the morning, when he saw a Benz crashed against a lamppost. He ran up to the car and found an old man passed out and bleeding all over. Struck by the smell of blood and liquor, the patrolman figured that the old man was a driver for some high official and rushed him to Pyongyang First Hospital. The doctor diagnosed a cracked skull and several broken ribs. The man was nearly dead. The hospital staff checked his pocket for identification, but they didn't find anything. The doctor spotted an expensive watch on his wrist. It was a solid gold Omega watch with "Kim Il-sung" stenciled in red lettering. The doctor guessed that the old man was a VIP and called Party Central. Men rushed in within five minutes and identified the old man as O Jin U and called Kim Jong-il. He hurried over to the hospital told the Party secretary at the hospital, "You must keep him alive. Get the best doctors. Bring foreign doctors. Give them all the money they ask for. Don't spare anything. And reward the patrolman who found and brought comrade O to the hospital." All the best doctors were brought in, and they concluded that it was best to ship him off to Moscow, which they did. Kim Jong-il spared nothing for him, and O managed to hang on to his life.

O recovered about a year later and went back to work as the minister of the People's Armed Forces. Moved by Kim Jong-il's devotion for him, he pledged his loyalty to Kim Jong-il. In 1992, he was promoted to marshal, the top post in the People's Army, and Kim Jong-il, not Kim Il-sung, presented O with the insignia. He is said to have shed tears as Kim Jong-il pinned the medal on him. By this time, Kim Il-sung had transferred his post as the supreme commander of the People's Army to Kim Jong-il.

Several significant events led to Kim Il-sung's transfer of military control to Kim Jong-il. The most important of these was the collapse of Communist regimes in the Eastern Bloc nations in 1989, countries like Poland, Czechoslovakia, and Hungary, not to mention the fall of the Berlin Wall. In Romania, people rose up against Nicolae Ceausescu, Kim Il-sung's close friend and ally. The Romanian army sided with the people, arrested Ceausescu, tried him in a military court, and executed him. This was a shocker for Kim Il-sung, according to Hwang, who was there with Kim Il-sung when the news came. Kim Il-sung was most concerned with the fact that the respective armies that should have defended the Party leadership had stood against the Party, or in the case of the Soviet Union, the army stood by and idly watched the August Coup.

Kim Il-sung was deathly afraid that the events in Eastern Europe and the Soviet Union would influence the North Korean political landscape. He felt the need to prepare for the worst and decided to hand over the military to Kim Jong-il while he was still living.

Four months after the failed coup in the Soviet Union, Kim Il-sung transferred control of the People's Armed Forces to Kim Jong-il as its supreme commander. The following year, Kim Il-sung revised the constitution with respect to the structure of the military. He created the National Defence Commission and made himself its chairman and Kim Jong-il the vice chairman and supreme commander. A year later, Kim Jong-il became chairman. Thus, Kim Jong-il took control of the military, intelligence, and the security [police] department.

What followed next was a wholesale shake-up of military personnel. It all began when a KGB operative leaked information to North Korean intelligence about a secret Soviet operation that was designed to "recruit" North Korean military personnel.

North Korea and the USSR had maintained a distant relationship beginning in the 1960s. Come 1985, North Korea was interested in modernizing its military and began expanding its military exchange program with the USSR. The Soviets welcomed the idea, because the USSR had been seeking to restore its influence in North Korea. Following a visit by Soviet military representatives in Pyongyang in 1985 for the fortieth anniversary of its liberation, 470 North Korean military officers went to the USSR to study in various military academies, including the air force, electronic warfare, and communication academy. At the same time, the North Korean army established in Pyongyang a four-year school called Mirim College, specializing in electronic warfare and invited forty high-ranking Soviet officers to teach there. The Soviets also set up a satellite communication center together with a listening post, Ramona Reconnaissance Base, in Ansan to monitor the American military activities in Okinawa. This brought the number of Soviet officers in North Korea to eighty. The Soviets proposed to dispatch a team of military representatives to Pyongyang in addition to the military attaché at the Soviet embassy. Concerned about the Soviet influence on the military, the North Korean authorities only allowed a limited number of Soviet representatives.

The Soviets' intentions were clear. They wanted to establish their influence in North Korea and decided to befriend high-ranking officers. The KGB initiated an operation with the officers studying in Moscow at the time. The students were receiving one hundred rubles a month for living expenses, and they supplemented their income by smuggling a variety of sundries, ginseng, and herb medicine. The KGB used this information to blackmail them. Also, the KGB found out that the students were not to engage in sexual relationships while they were studying overseas. Pyongyang presumed that the students who were in a sexual relationship compromised national secrets. Noting that the students lived alone without their spouses for a year or two, the agents laid traps for them with prostitutes. The majority of them fell victim to the KGB's enticement scheme. Sometime after, the KGB contacted the students one at a time and charged them with smuggling and womanizing. The KGB agents threatened to inform Pyongyang and the Soviet press about their behavior. The students found themselves hopelessly trapped.

Meanwhile, the Soviet military officers in Pyongyang began a parallel operation in concert with Moscow. In the end, the KGB "recruited" close to thirty students who had graduated with top honors. They were assigned to major posts in the People's Armed Forces upon their return to North Korea, including Lieutenant General Hong Kye-song, deputy chief of staff, and Brigadier General Kang Un-yong.

The brain trust in Pyongyang was not aware of this operation until the collapse of the Soviet Union, when a KGB operative leaked this information to North Korean intelligence. Section Chief Won Ung-hui launched an investigation and arrested several division commanders, who in turn confirmed the operation. Won Ung-hui immediately reported his findings to Kim Jong-il. Kim Jong-il said, "Soviet dogs or Chinese dogs are far more dangerous than Southern spies," and ordered a complete exposure of the operation. So began the bloodiest purge in the history of the People's Armed Forces, which lasted for two years from 1992 to 1994. In 1994 (the year Kim Il-sung died), about six hundred of the top military brass received discharge notices. Jo Myong-rok, then the chief air force commander, is said to have pleaded with Won Ung-hui, the investigator-in-charge and a close friend, "If you get rid of all the pilots, it will be the end of our air force." They took another look at the roster, so as not to decimate the entire air force.

Following this incident, all Soviet officers were expelled from North Korea. Consequently, the Soviet-North Korea exchange program came to an end. The North Korean armed forces modernization plan was temporarily halted.

According to former officers, this incident was reported to the outside world as a "conspiracy to commit a coup d'état," but in reality, it was an internal personnel shakeup.

When the purge was over, Kim Jong-il promoted 26 brigadier generals, 96 major generals, and 524 lieutenant generals to fill the void in the ranks. Kim Jong-il increased the benefits for these newly appointed generals, showering them with gifts on special holidays, such as Kim Il-sung's and Kim Jong-il's birthdays and New Year's. He also built a hospital exclusively for the generals and gave them other perks.

Taking control of the military was the most important item on his list as far as Kim Jong-il was concerned, evidenced by the military-first policy he would adopt later when he became the leader. Also, cooperation by the military was paramount for a smooth transition of power when Kim Il-sung died.

CHAPTER 6

DEATH OF KIM IL-SUNG

By the time Kim Il-sung died on July 8, 1994, Kim Jong-il was fully in charge, a fact little known outside of North Korea. That South Korea was unaware of this fact indicates either how poor its intelligence was or how successful Pyongyang was at putting on a show for the outside world. The conventional wisdom was that North Korea would collapse upon the death of Kim Il-sung, its sole ruler for forty-six years. South Korea and the United States were comparing North Korea to a disabled airplane on a crash course, and most of the debate centered on whether it would make a "soft landing" or come crashing down hard. Scholars and policymakers discussed contingency plans for both scenarios.

Just three weeks prior to Kim Il-sung's death, on June 16, former US president Jimmy Carter and his wife, Rosalyn, had visited Pyongyang to meet with Kim Il-sung to avert a certain crisis surrounding the weapons-grade plutonium processing plant at Yong Byon. During the meeting, Carter proposed a summit meeting between Kim Il-sung and then-South Korean president Kim Young-sam, on July 25. Both men agreed to the unprecedented summit, but the meeting never happened. Kim Il-sung died of a heart attack.

Kim Il-sung's secretary, Jon Ha-chol, recorded in his diary Kim Il-sung's final days as follows:[15]

---

[15] Ibid., pp.167-169, excerpt translated by John Cha

July 5, 1994

The great Su Ryong-nim supervised a meeting (at Myo Hyang Mountains) at an economics forum since this morning. Su Ryong-nim said that the continuous running of factories should increase production three-fold, and that we must solve the electricity shortage problem in order to achieve the Party's revolutionary economic goals. Everyone knew that the situation was bad, but no one had a solution for the electrical power problem. The meeting adjourned at noon.

The great Su Ryong-nim worked through the lunch hour without resting. At 1:10 PM, he called me in and asked me how much an oil-fired turbine generator cost.

I did not know the answer, and he instructed the Prime Minister to prepare the funds to import a turbine power generator and a boiler.

About thirty minutes later, he said he wanted to see if the Heavy Machinery Cooperative could build the turbine generator and wanted to send the head of the cooperative and a technician to the power generation plant.

He instructed me to arrange a helicopter for them right away. He called me several times to see if the helicopter had left and where it was, as well as how long it would take to acquire the turbine system.

At 9:06 PM, he told me that the head of the cooperative would not arrive today, and that they would have to leave early in the morning to attend the forum.

July 6, 1994

There were more participants today than the day before. The great Su Ryong-nim entered the meeting hall to an enthusiastic reception. Verifying that the head of the machinery co-op was in attendance, Su Ryong-nim asked whether it was possible to manufacture the turbine [domestically] if he provided the material and the parts for it. The head of the machinery cooperative said that it was possible.

The great Su Ryong-nim gave a historical speech, "About the Revolutionary Change in Constructing Socialist Economy." Su Ryong-nim clarified that the important elements in achieving the Party's revolutionary economic goals were electricity, chemical fertilizer, vinyl, cement, steel, and ships.

Sometime later, Su Ryong-nim looked around the meeting hall and said in a somber voice that the workers must raise their sense of responsibility and recognize the importance of their efforts in order to achieve economic success. Su Ryong-nim lamented that the economists were sitting around the office sharpening their talking skills rather than leading the revolutionary drive to remove the hurdles we were facing. He ended his speech. His face was grave and dark. His voice lacked energy.

The great Su Ryong-nim said that he felt cramped as he pounded his hand on his chest. He asked a helper to bring a cigarette. As he smoked the cigarette, he said in a worrisome tone, "I am taking up smoking again."

The meeting hall fell deadly silent. Holding the cigarette in his hand, he pointed out that the economists were going along without thinking, without a methodology, without due consideration for the masses. Su Ryong-nim instructed everyone that they should accomplish the JuChe ideals and its great will.

At 8:05 PM, he instructed the administrative department to formulate a plan to revive coal mining.

At 9:10 PM, he repeated his instruction to provide good-quality coal to cement factories.

July 7, 1994

It was a busy morning. I compiled the material from the meeting the day before along with the detailed plans from respective departments for expediting Su Ryong-nim's instructions.

At 4:09 PM Su Ryong-nim telephoned and asked about the progress of the plan, and I reported that the administration department and the national planning committee were working on the details.

At 5:25 PM Su Ryong-nim telephoned and asked about the death of a staff member's wife and the nature of her illness.

Ten minutes later, he called the office of the secretary and asked the staff about something.

At about ten at night, Su Ryong-nim called for the Party Secretary of the North Ham Gyong Province and asked him, "How is the food ration system doing? Are you providing enough food for the people?"

The Party Secretary replied, "There has been some shortage in supply up to now, but we're working on a plan to return to normalcy. You need not worry, sir."

Su Ryong-nim said in a worried tone, "You people keep telling me not to worry, but how can I not worry when we can't distribute rations on time for the people? You must have good crops this year and provide food supplies so they don't go hungry. Expedite the Na Jin development project and solve the food problem for the people in North Ham Gyong."

The following morning at two, with rain storming outside, Su Ryong-nim's great heart couldn't withstand the overexertion and stopped beating. I called out to him, but he didn't answer.

Needless to say, Kim Il-sung's sudden death was a shock for everyone, including Hwang Jang-yop. He made the following observation:[16]

In 1994, Kim Il-sung appeared healthy. But I noticed in meetings that he had weakened considerably and I had a feeling that he wouldn't last too much longer.

His hearing was getting worse. He had had eye surgery earlier in May and he was recuperating. He was exhausted from his meeting with Carter.

Kim Il-sung was quite excited in the meeting. He worked very hard to establish a rapport with Carter. Kim Il-sung was more excited as they finalized the July 25 date for his summit meeting with the South Korean president Kim Young-sam. Sitting in meetings with foreign dignitaries, I noticed that he was caught up in a fantasy that Korea was about to reunite, especially in light of Kim Jong-il's fabricated report that South Koreans worshipped Kim Il-sung. Accordingly, Kim Il-sung couldn't help but fall into the state of fantasy. It appeared that the excitement from Carter's visit and the impending summit meeting with the South caused additional pressure to his heart.

Carter's visit was a very significant event for Kim Il-sung, who for twenty years had sought to open a line of communication with the

---

[16] Ibid., p.171, excerpt translated by John Cha

United States. The meeting represented a turning point for him, an occasion to meet with an American leader face-to-face, as well as an opportunity to resolve the nuclear crisis.

When he met with Carter, Kim Il-sung said, "The basic problem between America and Joson [North Korea] is the lack of trust. To begin with, the first thing we have to do is establish an atmosphere of trust," and he added, "We have no capability to make nuclear weapons, nor do we need them. I've said this multiple times, but no one believes me."

He went on to say what the North really needed was nuclear energy, and that if the United States helped him with the construction of a light-water nuclear reactor, he would dismantle the gas-graphite reactors and return to the NPT (Non-Proliferation Treaty).

Kim Il-sung invited Carter to an outing on his yacht along the Dae Dong River, continuing their discussion. It was there that Carter suggested to Kim Il-sung a summit meeting with Kim Young-sam. Kim Il-sung replied, "I'll meet him without any preconditions."

Now eighty-two years old, he personally took charge of the preparations for the summit meeting that would never take place. He selected his favorite resort in the Myo Hyang Mountains for housing his counterpart from the South. He went there on July 7 and checked the condition of the guesthouse himself—its bedroom and bathroom—and he left instructions to fill the refrigerator with spring water. It was during this hot, busy day that he collapsed.

News of Kim Il-sung's death, released some thirty-four hours later, stunned the whole country. The entire nation mourned the passing of their "father," demonstrating anguish never seen before, while the rest of the world tried to guess what the future had in store for them.

Many experts predicted a general collapse due to a vacuum in leadership, but they could not have been more wrong. Kim Jong-il had been the real power behind the scenes for a decade or more.

Kim Jong-il tightened his grip on the society by strengthening the role of the military, while sealing off external communication and travels by Party officials. He was no longer referred to as the "Dear Leader," but the "Supreme Commander" (*choe goh saryong gwan,* the title he acquired in 1991). Party conferences and the People's Assembly were no longer convened. Instead, the military came to the forefront with Supreme Commander Kim Jong-il at the helm.

Nonetheless, 1994 was a year that can be characterized as one of crisis for Kim Jong-il. He survived the American threat to bomb the Yong Byon nuclear facility, his father's death, the food crisis, the electricity crisis, and the purge of the military officers connected with the KGB "recruit" operation.

He did have one bright moment, though. He emerged as a victorious leader because of the Geneva Agreement with the United States on October 21, in which North Korea agreed to give up the nuclear weapons program in exchange for two light-water nuclear reactors and five hundred thousand tons of heavy fuel oil per year.

He said to the members of the Party and the military: "Finally, Clinton has sent to me a guarantee to carry out the basic agreement [from Geneva] between Joson and the US. This is an unprecedented event in American history, in that an American president has issued practically a letter of surrender to a foreign leader. Obtaining a letter of surrender signed by an American president is the most brilliant achievement in our 5,000-year history. The worst traitor is Kim Young-sam. The puppets of the South are now interfering with our victory in Geneva. The Southern puppets are like dogs barking in the distance; the same with the Japanese. They have been issuing slanderous statements against our nuclear program, but they are quiet now.

"For now we should hold off using the anti-US slogans like 'US troops, get out of South Joson.' Don't even mouth those words. We will ignore it for a while and bring it up again when the time comes. In the meantime, we will focus our propaganda effort against the traitor Kim Young-sam. We will make a lot of noise about Kim Young-sam and his traitorous ways in opposing our agreement with the US. I'm certain that Kim Young-sam is suffering a case of anxiety because of the agreement."

Kim Jong-il was right about the South Korean anxiety. The South Korean press had a field day criticizing the United States for readily agreeing to the North Korean terms. Kim Young-sam and the South Korean officials felt left out of the negotiation process, while they ended up shouldering the bulk of the financial burden as the result of the agreement.

They were not very enthusiastic about the United States, their closest ally, entering into a relationship with North Korea to begin with. While the Geneva agreement made the news, the food crisis inside North Korea went without notice around the world. Kim Jong-il was aware of the food crisis, though. He gathered his top officials in the Information Department and told them, "The reason I am personally supervising newspapers, newswire, and broadcasting is because of the important role that mass communication plays in solving the most crucial problem, providing food for the people. Every day, radio and television are broadcasting my concerns for the people and all the effort that I am expending for the people. Comrades, you are to be commended for your work in 'spreading the greatness' of the Party [Kim Jong-il]. This current effort is fine for domestic use only, however. Externally, we must not reveal ourselves to the outside, but conceal ourselves as if Joson is inside the fog. We are to hide the politics of Kim Jong-il inside the fog."

He was intent on remaining mysterious to the outside world during this period, when the world was curious about the aftermath of Kim Il-sung's death. A year and a half passed by without an accurate picture of what was going on inside North Korea. Some experts erroneously opined that there was a power vacuum with no one in charge inside North Korea. They pointed to the fact that Kim Jong-il had not formerly succeeded the posts, party general secretariat, and presidium.

The official line, as directed by Kim Jong-il, was that North Korea was observing a three-year mourning period for Su Ryong, and that an "election" would only take place thereafter. Actually, he was busy restructuring the rank and file. There were a few Kim Il-sung loyalists who were suspicious of the circumstances surrounding Kim's death. They pointed to certain anomalies like the absence of cardiologists at Myo Hyang mountain resort, the delayed rescue helicopter, the presence of Kim Jong-il's personal staff in Kim Il-sung's room, and their confiscation of all the papers that belonged to Kim Il-sung, as suspicious.

It was no secret that there had been friction between Kim Il-sung and Kim Jong-il with respect to the reporting structure. Some members of the original partisan group were openly critical of Kim Jong-il's tendency to cut them off in the middle of speaking, never letting them finish what they were saying. "He never listens" was the common complaint to Kim Il-sung, who in turn ordered them to "come to me directly." This was how Kim Il-sung learned of the rice shortage, contrary to the false reports he had been receiving from Kim Jong-il. Hearing about the rice shortage problem, Kim Il-sung reportedly exploded in anger and gave an order to "immediately release the grains from the military reserve and distribute them to the people," but Kim Jong-il would have none of it. These "private" conversations behind his back bothered Kim Jong-il, and he meant to stay on top of it. He cleared out Kim Il-sung's personal staff and the last of the Kim Il-sung loyalists. He was grateful to his father's comrades for backing him, yet he wanted to keep his watchful eyes on them.

Then came the Yong Sung Spies incident, an event that would clear out all the holdovers from the Kim Il-sung era. The great purge began with Suh Gwan-hee, then the minister of agriculture, who otherwise was a loyal subject of the state and Kim Jong-il. He was made a scapegoat for the failed crops and was dragged to a busy intersection in Pyongyang and executed in front of a large crowd. "South Korean spy" was the justification for his execution, and many original partisans would suffer the same fate. They even dug up the remains of the former chairman of the agricultural commission of the Party, Kim Man-geum (dead since 1984), and shot him to pieces. Kim Jong-il praised the members of the Yong Sung group as heroes for rooting out the enemy spies.

People in general were made to believe that South Korea and the United States were taking advantage of the absence of Great Leader Kim Il-sung and conspiring to start a war. They also believed that South Korea and the United States were plotting to starve the people in preparation for war. It was in this atmosphere that the original partisans were "exposed" as South Korean spies. People were angry about the South Korean ploy to starve the masses and wanted to get to the bottom of it. As it turned out, the majority of those accused as spies were the remainders from Kim Il-sung's staff.

Kim Jong-il initiated the so-called *Shim Hwa Jo,* an identification system to add supplementary information in the ID card to include work experience, political history, and list of relatives. About eight thousand investigators were mobilized to facilitate the new system, with Chai Moon-dok in charge (under Jang Song-thaek, Kim's brother-in-law) and, in the process, they arrested and tortured many innocent people in search of "spies." Torturing became rampant, and one of the most painful tortures was called the "pigeon torture." Victims were hung off the ceiling by their hands and feet folded back together, which made their chests pop outward and turn white like the chest of a pigeon.

The interrogator would ask the victim, "You're a spy, right?"

If he said no, the interrogator kicked the "pigeon" in the chest once, cracking ribs, and asked again, "You're a spy, right?"

Most of the people gave up at this point and "confessed" that they were indeed spies, unable to withstand the pain of cracked ribs jabbing into their heart. The tough ones hung on the second time, but never made it past three kicks before they admitted that they were spies.

Chai's zealous investigators went overboard performing their duty, incarcerating altogether about twenty-five thousand people, many of whom were innocent of the charges, including Jang's political opponents. Jang had used the occasion to purge his opponents, who secretly taped the torture sessions and sent the recordings to Kim Jong-il, along with evidence of negative public sentiment. The situation deteriorated to the point that Kim Jong-il needed do something to calm the masses. He formed a commission to look into the matter, and the commission, with Jang Song-thaek in charge, "discovered" that the investigators were corrupt and usurped their authority for their own personal gain. He ordered Jang to discipline the investigators in question, and Jang promptly arrested most of the investigators and conducted the public execution of Chai, following a public airing of the recordings of the tortures. Thus, Kim Jong-il became "the hero who saved the country from corrupt officials."

This notorious *Shim Hwa Jo* incident would go down as the most vicious purge in North Korean history, according to those who witnessed it. If there were any questions about who was in charge of the country after Kim Il-sung died, the *Shim Hwa Jo* incident answered that question.

CHAPTER 7

THE FAMINE

Through *Shim Hwa Jo,* Kim Jong-il managed to—pardon the expression—kill many birds with one stone. He consolidated his power and calmed the public about the food shortage by placing the blame on South Korea and the United States. He carried out another purge in the process, but the real food shortage problem didn't go away.

The most startling news Hwang Jang-yop brought out of North Korea was about the famine and its 3 million victims. Sohn and I were in his office when he told us about the starvation. Like many, I had difficulty in believing that such a catastrophe was even possible in the first place. The thought of 3 million people starving to death didn't compute with me, and Hwang read what must have been a dumbfounded expression on my face. Imperceptibly, he shook his head and sighed, saying, "There's nothing worse than hunger."

I tried to recall what it was like being hungry. I replayed my life in reverse order, in search of the time and place that I had felt absolutely hungry. I finally traced myself back to my childhood during the Korean War, when my family was among the thousands of refugees awaiting a southbound train in the Seoul Railroad Station. It was dark inside the station, with people shouting and children crying all around me. I remember sitting on top of a load of bundles with my younger sister, waiting for my parents to come back from wherever they were.

A woman, whose face I can't recall, came by and gave us each a ball of rice as big as my fist, with sesame seeds sprinkled on it. The woman could have been my mother, for all I knew, but my focus was on the rice ball, not on her. I remember the sudden rush of elation and warmth inside me right then, followed by the sweetness that tingled all over me. I can say that that rice ball ruined my palate for the rest of my life, because I have not found anything tastier since then.

What's interesting, it was after I had eaten the rice ball that I felt hungry. I wanted more. Up to that point, I hadn't felt hungry per se. Looking back, I was in a state of numbness, beyond the normal pangs and the shakes that come with occasional meal-skipping for one reason or another. During wartime, people didn't "skip" meals, as if they had a choice in the matter. We ate when there was food; we didn't when there was not. More often than not, food was unavailable, simple as that. My memory of the three-day train ride to Busan does not include any food, but mostly sitting and dozing, lodged in between various shapes of bundles that were piled up to the ceiling.

According to the Merck medical library, biological organs become permanently damaged after eight to twelve weeks of starvation, followed by seizure and death. I can't imagine going eight weeks without food, and I hope I never will.

Back to my interview with Hwang at his office, I think I asked him, "Three million people? Out of 23 million population? That's one out of eight people."

He nodded and added, "Stationmasters at train stations had the roughest job. I talked to some of them. They told me that their main task was to collect and dispose of the dead bodies scattered around the station every morning—they were the people who had set out in search of food. They didn't make the train. Some of those who made the train died on the train."

A Chinese newswire service, Shin Hwa Sa, filed a report on December 18, 1997, which stated, "DPRK Agricultural Committee Deputy Commissioner Cha Rin-seok requested the Chinese government for assistance, quoting 2.8 million deaths due to natural disasters" (K.J. Sohn, Kim Jong-il Report, 2003, Badabooks). The newswire report, appearing nine months after Hwang's defection, seems to corroborate the number that was quoted to Hwang by the chief of statistics bureau a year earlier. Other studies, such as USIP (US Institute for Peace) Special

Report #51 (Andrew Natsios, August 1999), confirm these numbers as well:

> The KBSM [Korean Buddhist Sharing Movement] study plotted the home villages of the 1,679 refugees interviewed on a map of the 211 counties and then averaged the death rates by county, which were once again similar. The only exception is Pyongyang, which in the KBSM study showed a death rate one-third lower than the other counties—the lowest in the country. In both the Hopkins and KBSM surveys, death rates varied by age, gender, and profession rather than by geography. The Hopkins death rates, therefore, are a consistent, though conservative, estimate of the severity of the famine across the country.
>
> If anything, extrapolating the Hopkins death rates to the country as a whole understates rather than exaggerates the famine's severity. By deducting the 2 million people living in Pyongyang (the senior party cadre who have suffered least in the famine are heavily concentrated in the capital) and the 1.2 million soldiers, and then applying the 12 percent Hopkins rate of mortality to the 20 million people remaining, the total number of famine deaths would approach three million, the same number of deaths claimed by Hwang J[a]ng Yop. Thus, we have several independent studies that give credence to Hwang J[a]ng Yop's estimate.

The international community responded with food and grain. According to Andrew Natsios, "Sizable amounts of food have been imported into North Korea either as food aid, subsidized commercial sales, or cross-border barter trade between 1995 and 1999 primarily from China, Japan, South Korea, United States, and the European Union." As reported by the WFP (World Food Programme), food imports from all sources totaled the following amounts:

1995-1996:	903,374	Metric Tons
1996-1997:	1,171,665	Metric Tons
1997-1998:	1,321,528	Metric Tons

Much of the aid did not reach the downtrodden in time, however, especially in the outlying areas of the country, such as North Ham

Kyung Provinces. Relief workers returning from North Korea observed that rice was rotting in warehouses due to poor storage and/or lack of transportation. This was confirmed by a missionary worker who had spent considerable time in Pyongyang. She told me, "I saw the rice rotting at the bottom of the pile in one of the government warehouses."

There were reports that the bulk of the aid was used in rotating grain stock for the military, replacing the old grains with the new, and recycling the old rice for general distribution. The Party cadre, the leaders in the Workers' Party, in the meantime, sold the aid goods in the marketplaces that had sprouted up since 1994, when the government ration system became virtually defunct, except for the Pyongyang region.

The international aid effort didn't seem to benefit the outlying areas, where they needed the help the most. A defector from an outlying village in Ham Kyung province described to me his experience:

> You walk down the village road, pass by a neighbor's house like you do every day. If you see smoke rising up their chimney, you know they're all right. If you don't see smoke coming out of their chimney for several days, you know they're all dead.

At a recent lunch in Seoul with a group of defectors, the menu included a side dish made out of squash. I delved into the squash roasted to golden brown, saying over and over, "This is wonderful, this is wonderful."

A young fellow seated across the table frowned, forcing a smile, and said, "I can't stand the sight of the squash; I don't even want to smell it."

I asked him, "Why not?"

He replied, "I had squash day and night for years. That's all I had. Squash stew, fried squash, boiled squash, baked squash, squash gruel … I don't remember eating anything else."

I stopped eating the squash. It didn't taste good any longer.

The young fellow said, "In retrospect, I was fortunate. I had squash to eat, at least."

I understood what he meant. He felt fortunate that he had managed to live to tell his story.

A minister from Chicago whom I'd met some time ago told me about his congregation in a church in Pyongyang. "These people feel very fortunate to eat one bowl of corn gruel a day. It's a feast for them. They would hold hands and thank God for the meal. It is remarkable how they survive. Their urine has no smell and their feces look like rabbit dung, you know those little pellets. Still, they go on and keep their faith in God. They're truly remarkable."

The good minister, who appeared to weigh over two hundred pounds, went on like this, and I failed to understand his twisted logic in lavishing his praise for the starving people. He ought to have been telling them that humans were meant to eat three meals a day, not praise them for their ability to subsist on one bowl of gruel a day.

My mother used to say that being hungry was part of life in her youth. She remembered the times when pebbles on the ground appeared appetizing: "When you're hungry, you don't think of anything else. Pebbles look like cookies. Intellectually, you know that you can't chew or digest them, but you don't care. You feel as though you could sink your teeth into them. You see a mound of sand, and soon, you begin to wish that it was a mound of rice. You begin to imagine that you're scooping it up in your hand and shoving it in your mouth. You know that you can't eat sand; that your stomach can't handle it, but you find yourself fighting the urge to scoop it up into your hands and eat it. Sometimes you see little kids eating dirt. They can't control the urge."

I have never seen my mother throw away food. It made her sick to see people waste food. When we went out to restaurants, she always brought home leftovers. She had lived with food shortages for so many years that saving food became second nature. All of her friends and relatives were the same way, and when Mother got together with them, they reminisced about the old days, those hungry days.

One of them would say, "I always felt hungry. I don't ever remember not being hungry. I used to imagine how wonderful it would be to be full. I'd imagine eating until my stomach would burst."

They would chime in, laughing, "Yes, yes. I was the same way."

Mother would add, "I was twenty years old when I tasted a *bulgogi* barbecue for the first time in my life. I had always heard about how delicious it was. And it was."

They laughed heartily again, but the humor was lost to me. I didn't understand why they were laughing about being hungry or tasting *bulgogi* beef for the first time. They seemed to be enjoying the walk down their own memory lane, such as it was, and I felt out of place. I surmised that I needed to have been there with them during their youth in order for me to enjoy their humor.

Mother continued, offering an explanation for my behalf, "*Bulgogi* was such a treat then; only the rich people could have it. But now I don't care for it anymore. Our generation has had the worst time when it came to food. We've gone through a lot in our lifetime: the Japanese rule, World War II, the Korean War. Most of the food went to feed soldiers, leaving very little for the rest of the people to fight over. So you see, wars mean hunger. I may be wrong, but I bet that more people died of hunger than by bullets and bombs."

That is a sobering thought—more people dead from starvation than bullets and bombs. I wonder if there is a study to substantiate such a theory. The war had wrought about 4 million dead civilians, no one is sure of the number, and it would be impossible to account for each person and his or her cause of death.

In a war, nobody really cares how people perish. The weak have no voice. They are mere victims of a "higher cause." Just like the victims in North Korea who are now suffering starvation, fifty-seven years after the war. There is no explanation for such a plight in this day and age, especially when well-to-do neighbors such as South Korea, China, and Japan surround North Korea. It seems absurd that 3 million people would be allowed to die of starvation so close by.

According to Hwang, Kim Jong-il doesn't share these sentiments. He offered this explanation: "My sense is that Kim Jong-il doesn't feel any urgency about the starvation issue. He feels that he has larger issues to deal with, and in his own mind, he feels that the sacrifice is warranted. He is more interested in preserving his power."

CHAPTER 8

KIM JONG-IL'S PRESERVATION OF POWER

K im's priority issues center around preservation of his power base, which by his definition, is synonymous with the country's integrity itself. He often refers to himself as "fatherland," meaning that what's good for him is good for the fatherland. By the same token, his enemies are the enemies of the fatherland. And he deposes anyone who challenges his authority as the enemy of the fatherland. That's how he manages to stay in control of power even after the catastrophic famine that claimed 3 million lives.

Hwang added, "He doesn't feel responsible for the famine. He believes that the responsibility falls on the economists. The only thing he is concerned about is *Kim Il-sung's Ten Principles* and compliance thereof." The Ten Principles call for absolute respect and obedience to the great leader Kim Il-sung and, by extension, supreme commander Kim Jong-il. That is the basis for all of his policies.

In this chapter, we will examine what kept him in power and how he preserved it. Specifically, we will address his "military-first (*Songun pronounced Son Goon*) policy," his manipulation of people and information, and his health.

Military-First Policy

By employing a "military-first" policy immediately after the death of Kim Il-sung, Kim Jong-il effectively declared martial law for the entire country, with him as the commander-in-chief, whereby military rules take precedence over any civilian regulations. Under this policy, the military behaves like a nation of its own, independent of the rest of the country. It has its own farms, distribution system, trading and transportation systems, factories dedicated to military goods production, and scientific research facilities. The military also manages the country's electric power plants and large-scale construction projects that require a large labor force, such as building highways, railroad facilities, harbor facilities, and underground military bases.

Of these, building and maintaining underground bases receive the most attention because of their vast scale. Bombers, fighter airplanes, missiles, tanks, cannons, trucks, ammunition dumps, command headquarters, power generators, living quarters, and electronics equipment are stored underground. These underground complexes are vast, and they are the result of the bombing raids by the United States during the Korean War. Kim was ten years old when the war began, living in Jilin, away from the raining bombs, but he most likely grew up hearing horror stories from his father and those who had fought in the war. The UN forces had driven his father, Kim Il-sung, to the Chinese border, where he had to take refuge on the shores of the Yalu River. Then the Chinese army joined the war and saved him and his fleeing troops from certain destruction. No doubt Kim Jong-il inherited from his father a sense of hatred toward the UN troops, mainly the US bombers that devastated Pyongyang and other cities in North Korea.

It is, therefore, not surprising that he would invest heavily in underground facilities. For instance, his command center in Cheol Bong Li is a huge bunker beyond comprehension. A Japanese monthly magazine, *Modern,* carried an article about the facility in its June 2003 issue. An Yong-chol, a former officer in the North Korean army, described the facility in very illuminating detail:[17]

---

[17] K.J. Sohn, *Kim Jong-il Report,* (Seoul: Bada Publishing, 2003), p.255, excerpt translated by John Cha

The super secret command post Cheol Bong Li base is located under the mountain called Guk Sa Bong (1,456 feet above sea level), which is about 9.4 miles northeast of Pyongyang Plaza.

There are two entrances to the base, one at Moon Li and the other at Jang Su Won reservoir. Whichever the entrance, you go down about 39 feet and reach a tunnel that is 29.5 feet wide, 14.76 feet high, and 1,968 feet long. [About five and a half football fields in length.] The walls are heavily lined with anti-radiation material. This is the underground command center for the military. It has two levels, and the upper level has nine war rooms.

One of those rooms is called the Observation Room, which is equipped with screens that constantly show images from the Russian spy satellite and television broadcast from all over the world.

Fifteen operators man the post around the clock. The images are duplicated in all the bases down the line to the brigade level, the regiment level, the battalion level, and the company level command posts.

The lower level has sixteen offices earmarked for the top officials. Kim Jong-il's room is the fourth one on the right, around 2,150 square feet, equipped with a large screen and the latest computers. In the event that Cheol Bong Li comes under attack, Kim Jong-il has a separate emergency escape route. The emergency tunnel is connected to Nampo Harbor on the western seaboard about fifty miles away. There is another emergency exit that leads to the command post for the defence department under Baik Jok Mountain that is located about 3.1 miles away. There's a power station in the tunnel as well. Also, under the mountains to the northeast of the command post there is a base for the tank corps dedicated to guard Kim Jong-il. They guard all the main points in the facility.

Hwang Jang-yop corroborated the presence of such a major underground facility. He wrote in his memoirs, "Beginning in 1973, I was working on a manuscript at a resort in Cheol Bong Li. There was a reservoir in between mountains thick with pine forest. It was the first resort built by the Party Central, a shabby house with only a few rooms. But it was a perfect place for me. About one year later, Kim Jong-il telephoned me and said that he was planning a major construction project at the Cheol Bong Li resort and recommended that I use a resort in Wonsan. At that time, they were digging a tunnel deep in the mountain. I surmised that Kim was referring to the same project. Looking back on the nature of the construction project, I thought they were building a special resort for possible emergency use."

The use of these underground facilities provides insight into Kim's modus operandi. In March 2003, it was reported that Kim Jong-il had not been seen in public for forty-three days. It was eventually discovered that he had spent time at the underground bunker Cheol Bong Li near Pyongyang, watching and analyzing television broadcasts about the American invasion of Iraq. He and his military leaders were no doubt concerned about whether or not US forces could roll across North Korea in the same way they had in Iraq.

Another underground facility called "Area 21" in the middle of Pyongyang also is a command post for Kim Jong-il to use in wartime, according to Ri Young-kuk, who had served Kim Jong-il as a bodyguard for ten years. It is large enough to house all the Party cadres as well as the officials from the Executive Department. Heavily guarded by fifteen hundred guards and five hundred mounted police to maintain its secrecy, the bunker covers an area of about two miles square. It is connected to downtown Pyongyang and other cities via subway trains. The area is heavily fortified with reinforced concrete, strong enough to withstand a nuclear blast.

It is difficult to determine how extensive these underground facilities are. Apparently, the underground network is extensive enough for Hwang to quip that "in a word, you can say that entire North Korea is one large bunker." Hwang said, "[Kim Jong-il] means to keep intact as much infrastructure as possible in the event of a war."

Another war in the Korean Peninsula is unthinkable, but if a war came to pass, he mostly likely would choose one of these bunkers to live in. He would conduct the war through the extensive computer network installed to communicate with his field generals. He would be surrounded by his personal security force, one of his favorite military units. His personal security force and the anti-South task force are his favorite units.

SPECIAL FORCES

Kim Jong-il loved covert operations, and his personal security force and anti–South task force unit ran these programs for him. Anti–South operations have been going on since the Kim Il-sung days and continue today. Secrecy is key to the success of these operations, and Kim Il-sung always emphasized the importance of absolute secrecy when it came to anti–South activities. Kim Jong-il, who took over the supervision of the anti–South operations around 1979, was just as vigilant about maintaining secrecy, if not more.

Secrets do not remain secret forever. There are a good number of former operatives and agents who have lived to tell the innermost workings of the operations. In the early 1980s, Kim Jong-il consolidated all the departments related to anti–South operations and built a new facility called "Building 3," including the notorious "Office 35." This is where the Rangoon bombing (1983) was planned and directed. This bombing killed seventeen South Korean officials, including members of the South Korean cabinet, the ambassador to Burma, and staff members of Chun Doo-hwan's government. Chun Doo-hwan, then president of South Korea, and his wife were late getting there and escaped the attack.

Office 35 also planned and executed the kidnapping of South Korean actress Choi Eun-hee and her husband, Sheen Sang-ok. In 1987, Office 35 planned and directed the explosion of a Korean Air passenger airplane, which killed everyone aboard. The reason they assign numbers to various departments and sections is to keep everyone guessing about what they do. For instance, Offices 38 and 39 of the Party manage Kim Jong-il's Swiss bank accounts. Office 35, sometimes called the "External Communication Department," is responsible for all covert anti–South activities, the infiltration and coordination of field agents, terrorism, and inciting social unrest. Better known to outsiders is the "Department of Re-unification Front," which openly advocates the Party's points of view in conjunction with various groups located in Japan, the United States, and Canada.

Building 3 is largely staffed by the graduates of Kim Jong-il School of Military Politics. These students are named "Combatants" because of the intense combat training they undergo. The school is located in Hak San-li, the Hyung Je Mountain region of Pyongyang, situated on 163 acres. Originally, this school was under the supervision of the Party

Central Committee until 1992, when the name was changed to Kim Jong-il University of Military Politics. The five-year school produces about one hundred to two hundred graduates annually. The school's curriculum consists of ideological training (40 percent); combat skills, shooting, and physical training (40 percent); and photography, driving, and other practical skills (20 percent).

In addition, students learn about the merits of honorable suicide as the final solution in the event they are compromised, which, according to a former student, they become used to and accept by the time they graduate. In September 1996, eleven covert agents killed themselves as they were fleeing from their submarine that was grounded on the East Sea shore in South Korea. The same unit planned and executed the daring operation of sneaking Scud missiles to Iraq during the Gulf War in 1991. Kim Jong-il ordered Oh Geuk-ryul, then commander of the unit, to send the missiles to Iraq in the name of the Party. Coalition forces had, at that time, sealed off all routes to Iraq, and they were faced with an impossible task.

The unit had twenty ships available, ranging from four thousand tons to forty thousand tons, supposedly oceangoing freighters designated for international trading. They selected two of the most experienced vessels for the job, and three days later they loaded the ships with missile parts and embarked from the port of Wonsan. The US authorities were already aware of the plans to smuggle the missiles, and the coalition forces mobilized their search operations for these two ships at high seas. The ships changed their route to Syria and managed to slip through the coalition's dragnet and unload the Scud missiles there. The entire crew was rewarded with a hero's welcome when they returned home. Kim Jong-il praised them, "Only *my* soldiers could have accomplished this."

The agents have proven their toughness over the years, and Kim Jong-il is credited with creating and building their training program. In 1979, when three agents successfully escaped from South Korea despite a tight military dragnet, Kim Jong-il praised them, "Comrades, the reason you were able to return safely was because of your unending loyalty to the Party and your ironman condition. From now on, I want to strengthen the training for all the combatants, so they are able to run forty to eighty kilometers a night." From that point on, the field combatants began training with twenty-kilogram sandbags strapped on their backs. Beginning in 1984, non–combat agents and intelligence analysts were required to do physical training as well, because of an incident that had occurred in Nepal. A non-combat agent in Nepal was exposed, forcing him to abandon his post. It took him forty days to get back to Pyongyang, mostly walking his way through three countries. Kim Jong-il praised him as a true hero and required all the non-combat agents to do physical training, running four kilometers every day, twenty kilometers on weekends, and forty kilometers at month's end.

The Party's strategy department has dozens of satellite posts, six of them dealing with anti-South operations. Of the six satellite posts, two of them involve overland infiltration and the remaining four, ocean routes. These posts also function as training grounds for various infiltration methods. Agents wearing a twenty-kilogram backpack run forty kilometers in three hours, swim eight kilometers, over and under water, submerge in a frozen river for over thirty minutes, and train in hand-to-hand combat against fifteen to twenty opponents.

The Strategy Department also has communication posts. Post 4.14 is one of them, located in the Moran-bong region, Pyongyang. It has thirteen buildings over 1.6 acres, surrounded by a concrete wall two meters high. This is where they collect and analyze all the communication data related to South Korea. They also exchange communication with their respective agents stationed in South Korea and overseas. Constructed in 1965, this post houses three thousand agents. An additional two thousand agents are posted in the countryside as well.

Kim Jong-il's personal security force is also a secret operation. The outside world got their first glimpse of Kim Jong-il's personal security force in July 2001 when he visited Russia on the Trans-Siberia Railroad. Constantine Pulikovski, a Russian diplomat who accompanied him for twenty-four days, described the trip in his book, *Orient Express,* published in Moscow in 2002:

> I regularly met Kim Jong-il in the car 1, which was a gift from Josef Stalin to Kim Il-sung, the first leader of the Democratic People's Republic of Korea. About fifty sharpshooters dressed in special gear rode in two passenger cars. At every stop, they would position themselves on overpasses and along the railroad track in a defensive stance. Some special guards worked undercover and out of sight.
>
> Kim Jong-il's special train was equipped with his sleeping car, a conference car, dining car, and a storage

car with two Mercedes Benz's inside. The entire train was luxuriously decorated, and the atmosphere was very cordial. The conference car had two large screens, one a movie screen and the other, with an electronic map constantly showing our location. The train was equipped with a satellite dish and each car had a computer hooked to a common network... I didn't ask Kim Jong-il why he rode the train instead of flying. But he told me indirectly during our conversation that he wanted to trace his father's footsteps through Russia.

By invoking his father, he reminded the Russians of the glory days of Stalin and Kim Il-sung, when the international communist movement was alive and well. After the trip, Kim Jong-il sent a telegram to Vladimir Putin: "I sincerely wish that you would accomplish what the communists of Russia failed to accomplish." Kim Jong-il was taking a shot at Putin's predecessors for compromising with the Western Bloc. At the same time, he was telling the Russians that he was a true communist to the end. Be that as it may, Kim Jong-il did leave a mark in more ways than one across the Russian landscape from Siberia to Moscow and St. Petersburg.

While he traveled across Russia, the country's normal railroad traffic was interrupted, which annoyed the local residents. The Russian authorities would stop all traffic several hours before and after Kim Jong-il's train pulled into a station. In addition, the Russian police force posted an officer every one hundred meters alongside the railroad track, ninety-three thousand men altogether.

When the train stopped at the Habvrosk station for thirty minutes, the station was emptied and kept dark to keep the public out of the station. In St. Petersburg, Leningrad, and Omsk, they closed all the shops and sealed off building rooftops around the station.

This trip gave the world a glimpse into his security forces, but it wasn't until Ri Young-kuk, Kim Jong-il's former bodyguard defected in 2000 that more specific details were revealed. He wrote a book entitled, *I Was Kim Jong-il's Personal Bodyguard,* published by Shidae Jongshin in 2002, containing "by far the most detailed description of Kim Jong-il's daily routine" according to Hwang Jang-yop.

> Section 5 of the Party Central Committee Organizational Guidance Department is responsible for Kim Jong-il's safety, and it only acts on Kim Jong-il's direct command ... The personal security force is organized in various layers, or lines

of defense. For instance, the first layer is the bodyguard unit. The bodyguards follow him wherever he goes and relay his messages to other units. The second layer is taken up by the event management unit when he attends a state event or goes on an inspection tour in the countryside. This unit wears military uniform and civilian clothes interchangeably. The mobile event staff holds down the third position. The fourth is the national security bureau, and the fifth, the police department. The local security bureau brings up the sixth column, and the local police department, the seventh. The strategy department plans for all the labor and materials needed and finances the events and inspection tours. The rear service unit takes care of the food and staples necessary for the security force.

The security system is deliberately complicated, and the rules governing personnel are just as complex. Ri Young-kuk explained the daily routine and requirements for a security agent:

> Bodyguards must always be pleasant. If his expression is dark, he is not allowed to pull his duty that day due to his unstable emotional state ... Only the commissioned bodyguards over thirty can get married, and his partner must be a woman from Section 5 of the Party Central: a typist, telephone operator, or administrative staff.
>
> When he applies for marriage, his supervisor puts 20 photos upside down on the table for him to pick. If he refuses to marry the one he picked, then he has to wait another two years to draw straw again, at which time, he has to marry the one he picks. He is allowed to go home once a week. The Party Central provides a house, about 1,200 square feet, located in the area surrounding Kim Jong-il's office.
>
> The system is designed to protect the inner secrets, and the security personnel are paid four times the average worker, plus receiving special perks with respect to their children's education. Security personnel cannot participate in public events because their identity would be compromised, as would the size of the force. All information on security matters is sealed off to the public.
>
> For instance, the security personnel do not show up on any record, have no identification number or card. It is as if they do not exist.

Manipulation of People

Kim Jong-il was masterful in the art of manipulating people. He knew when and how to reward people and when to punish them. He inherited this talent from his father. If he decided that someone was worthless, Kim expelled him from the Party, meaning certain death to the individual's political career.

On the other hand, for those who he believed were worth reviving, he gave them a second chance by "re-educating them about the revolutionary ideals." He assigned them (with one day's notice) to farms, mines, factories, or distant posts in the countryside and examined their re-education process. His standard for examination was their loyalty. If they proved their loyalty to the satisfaction of Kim Jong-il, they were reinstated in their previous position. If they were deemed disloyal, they were sent to a political correction center.

Choe Kwang, the joint chief of staff, was purged in January 1969. He was sent to a factory in the South Hwang Hae Province until 1976, when Kim Jong-il was convinced of his unswerving loyalty. Kim Jong-il reinstated him and appointed him to the office of chairman of the People's Committee of South Hwang Hae Province. Subsequently, Choe was promoted to the position of chief of staff, following Oh Geuk-ryul in February 1988.

Often, loyalty and devotion were given priority over all other considerations. One incident in 1987 illustrates how important loyalty is regarding affairs of state.[18]

> In early 1987, Kim Bong-gon, the Ambassador to Lebanon, was caught smuggling several thousands of Seiko watches at the airport in Cairo, Egypt. A major Egyptian newspaper reported this incident, and the Egyptian State Department expressed their disappointment. The incident was reported to Kim Jong-il, who fumed, "Bring him back. He's a traitor to the fatherland." The entire Foreign Service Department thought that Kim Bong-gon was headed for political prison for sure because Kim Jong-il had referred to him as a "traitor." Immediately, Kim Bong-gon was recalled to Pyongyang for interrogation. Kim Bong-gon did well to

---

[18] K.J. Sohn, *Kim Jong-il Report,* (Seoul: Bada Publishing, 2003), p.318, excerpt translated by John Cha

display his devotion to the Party by confessing, "I entered into a risky business because I wanted to prepare a cash gift for the comrade leader on his birthday on February 16."

The interrogators at the Organizational Bureau reported this back to Kim Jong-il. Kim Jong-il instructed, "Don't expel him from the Party." Kim Bong-gon was promoted one classification and remained in the Foreign Service Department. He was compensated for his loyalty to Kim Jong-il.

In this incident, Kim Bong-gon escaped certain punishment because of his loyalty to Kim Jong-il, despite the embarrassment he caused for North Korea by getting caught with thousands of Seiko watches. Kim Jong-il's quirks with respect to his handling of people is legendary, especially his tendency to make snap decisions in personnel matters. His impromptu appointments generally involve deputy directors in all sectors. The following is a well-known anecdote in the Ministry of Foreign Affairs.[19]

One day in April 1988, the telephone rang at two in the morning. The manager on duty answered the call. The telephone operator's tense voice came on the line.

"This is our Dear Leader's office calling. Who is this?"

"Ah, this is the Third Protocol Officer."

"Please hang up the phone and wait."

The phone rang again in five minutes. "Our Dear Leader is on the line for you."

The Third Protocol Officer stood up at attention, holding the receiver with his two hands. "It's an honor to take a call from our Dear Leader, sir."

Kim Jong-il spoke, "Third Protocol Officer, I have a question about the foreign dignitaries visiting us currently. Do you know what they did yesterday and their reaction?"

"Yes, sir, Comrade Leader." The officer replied confidently, for he was coordinating the itinerary of the visitors. "They visited the West Sea Lock facility yesterday. Their delegation leader repeatedly praised the facility, and how it reflects the greatness of the comrade leader. Deputy

---

[19] K.J. Sohn, *Kim Jong-il Report* (Seoul: Bada Publishing, 1993), pp.319, excerpt translated by John Cha

Director Kim Chae-suk instructed me to file a full report by fax later this morning, sir."

"You're very sharp, *dongmu* [literally translated, friend comrade], you're fit to be an ambassador."

Next day, the Third Protocol Officer was appointed ambassador to a Scandinavian country.

Sung Hye-rang, writer and Kim Jong-il's former sister-in-law, has made her observations about Kim Jong-il's manipulative personality in her book *Wisteria House (Deung Namu Jip)*. Her observations explain Kim's abrupt style:

> He [Kim Jong-il] has a sixth sense about what is true and what isn't. My sister Hye-rim (Kim's first wife) and I knew that we were better off telling him the truth no matter what the situation.
>
> He is a cultured man and respects knowledge. He enjoys beauty. I'd see his face relax comfortably when he saw something humble and unpretentious. On the other hand, if he saw something shabby and gaudy, he'd yell unmercifully.
>
> He hated anything excessive, whatever it was. He jeered at imperfections. Had he grown up in a poor home, he would have been an artist.
>
> He grew up on his own in a place surrounded by unlimited power and luxury without any interference from anyone, motherly love and care.
>
> I think he has inherited some good points—generosity and a warm heart. He was always considerate and wanted to do well by others. His extreme, harsh personality makes him seem like a bad human being, and I thought that this was a result of his environment. Unlimited power, lack of education, the absence of a mother, and that totalitarian society produced his personality. Contradictions in his personality can be confusing and incomprehensible at times.

She saw him close-up while she lived with her sister, Hye-rim, Kim Jong-il's first wife. The sisters were inseparable. Hye-rang, the *onni*, or older of the two, looked after Hye-rim from her youth through her stardom as a movie actress and a North Korean heartthrob and, finally, as Kim Jong-il's wife. No doubt Hye-rang was the first to know about

Hye-rim's discreet love affair with Kim Jong-il, which began in 1968, followed by a secret marriage in 1969 and the birth of Kim Jong-il's first son in 1971.

Hye-rang lived with Hye-rim through her glorious years and subsequent depression that began in 1974 and lasted until 1996, when Hye-rang defected. Hye-rang knew Kim as a romantic, artist, husband, and father. She adds that "he has the uncanny ability to tell if someone is telling a lie." In her interview with *Time* magazine in July 2003, she said, "If he feels that someone has told him a lie or if he feels betrayed, he can be very dangerous. He really hates liars."

Lee Han-young, Hye-rang's son, writes about a guard named Su Hon in his memoir, *Kim Jong-il's Royal Family*. (Shidae Jongshin, 2004)

> [Su Hon] was responsible for guarding the residential compound. In 1978 he was sacked because of his illicit affairs inside Kim Jong-il's limo. Kim Jong-il is crazy about cars. He has a number of cars in the residential compound as well as his office.
>
> He has Mercedes Benz 450 in black and green, several Cadillac's, Rolls Royce, and Benz 600. There were Jong-nam's cars, a Benz and a Cadillac.
>
> Su Hon would take these cars for a cruise at night, armed with expensive stockings and Japanese cosmetics for his secret rendezvous with actresses.
>
> Once in a while, Kim Jong-il would look for him at night, only to find that Su Hon was not available. Kim Jong-il suspected that something was wrong, and one day, he summoned Su Hon and asked, "What are you doing sneaking out with my car? I know everything, so tell me."
>
> Fearing that Kim Jong-il already knew everything, he confessed to his misconduct. He was never seen again.

Kim Jong-il's reputation as a truth monger went beyond his residential compound. At a meeting in his office attended by the various department heads, including the chief of police and the chief of the organizational department, Kim Jong-il admonished the chief of police and his department for not filing accurate reports. "I like accurate, true reports. All of you know Ernst Kaltenbrunner, the chief of the SS during the Nazi era. When he made his reports to Hitler, he always was simple and accurate. At times when Himmler, the number two man, exaggerated or altered any information on behalf of Hitler, Kaltenbrunner would correct his superior. I need bold people like that. I want you to be like Kaltenbrunner." The men scrambled around for books and movies on Kaltenbrunner and studied him and wrote reports on him.

These anecdotes help us understand his complex personality and by extension his management style. There are as many interpretations of his personality as there are witnesses. It is very interesting that people who have come in close contact with him have completely different views of him.

Hwang Jang-yop believed that Kim Jong-il was a liar. Sung Hye-rang provides some insight into his personality as a man, as does her son, Lee Han-young.

Kenji Fujimoto, who had had a chance to observe Kim Jong-il for thirteen years as his personal chef, said in his interview with *Chosun Daily News* in 2003, "Kim Jong-il ordinarily never shows off. He is a warm person with many hobbies, and always wears a smile. But when someone fails to report an important item, or when something goes wrong, he yells and screams into the telephone like a madman. I have often witnessed this. He has no qualms about chewing out senior officials, no matter who they are. Once I saw him throw a stainless napkin holder at Jang Song-thaek, his brother-in-law. After his father died, Kim Jong-il spent a lot of time alone in his room."

Ri Young-kuk, former bodyguard, saw different sides of Kim Jong-il as well. "He is generally impatient and sly. There's more to him than his pleasant exterior. Inside, he is always scheming, making secret plans. And he is very clever about planning escape routes in case things go wrong. There are two sides to him, always. He is not a good listener. He likes to take care of things on his own and is extremely cruel toward those who disagree with him. Many people have lost their lives trying to point out problems to him.

"He used to say, 'When the enemy gives you a problem, yell louder than them, and they'll back down.' But he often worried that, if the Panmunjom opened up, the American troops would invade Pyongyang in forty-five minutes."

South Korean filmmaker Sheen Sang-ok and his actress wife, Choi Eun-hee, had an opportunity to observe Kim up close while they lived in North Korea for eight years. They were, according to Kim Jong-il, "invited guests," but in reality, were abducted to make films for him.

They made a daring escape while traveling in Vienna and returned to the South. They managed to bring with them a sixty-minute tape of Kim's voice that they had recorded in secret, which explains why he had "brought" the couple to the North:

Kim: Eh, the first thing in the North-South relations is the cultural exchange, cultural cooperation, that's what I think. Already, people were going back and forth on their own accord, and I asked whether there was a way for you, Director Sheen, to visit us on your own, and we discussed this among our comrades, and at that time, our people in Hong Kong sent word that you were traveling to Hong Kong, uh, that your older brother was there.

Eh, we learned that he was looking to make movies in Hong Kong because he couldn't make movies in the South. So then at that time, we knew about your brother, and so we decided to find out about you, what your plans were. So we looked at all the films, all the film materials, that was when Choe Ik-kyu was the manager then, and when I asked him who was the best director in the South, he said, "Director Sheen. First of all, his family originally is from the North, ha ha ha ... Next, his emotion, his emotional condition was down, long under Park Chung-hee, he would not stay long in the South." You were trying to go outside to do your work, that's the word we got, through your older brother.

Sheen: That's when they refused to renew my permit [for my film company] in the South....

Kim: Right, right. Eh, so we said fine. Then we should bring him over, but we said, it would be tough to bring this man. It would be too hard to bring this man alone, so we said we needed to entice him with something. So we brought your wife to entice you. (Laughter) My intent at that time, it was, I wanted to show how a director from the South could come to our republic and make movies with real freedom, with no worries whatsoever. That was my true intent ...

What comes through in the recording is that Kim Jong-il talks fast and doesn't give Sheen a chance to reply or talk. He rambles, jumps from one thought to another, which some scholars attribute to his tendency to think faster than he can speak. A team of neurologists, psychologists, and sociologists from Ewha University analyzed his recording and observed that he was an emotional and passionate person with an artistic bent. Second, he is impatient and self-centered. Third, he has a conflicted personality, which most likely stems from his inability to exercise his artistic freedom under the rigid, socialistic structure. This conflicted state makes everyone around him very uncomfortable.

Professor Cho Young-hwan from Sogang University offers his analysis: Kim Jong-il is smart, honest, and makes quick decisions. On the other hand, he is anti-social, moody, and carries an unstable self-image. In describing this condition, Professor Cho traces back to Kim's infancy, when his mother relied on the childcare centers to look after the baby, i.e., breastfeeding by a surrogate, while she performed her duties with the Soviet Union's Far East Eighty-eighth Regiment. His lack of mother's attention and milk would impact his life, so the theory goes, resulting in him blaming his father for his mother's death and transferring his hatred to his stepmother, Kim Song-ae. He chose Sung Hye-rim as his first wife because she reminded him of his mother.

Professor Cho associates this antisocial tendency and abrupt personality with Kim Jong-il's lonely childhood. He often interrupts a music band in the middle of a performance for no reason. He routinely switches subjects in the middle of a conversation. Professor Cho summarizes Kim Jong-il's personality traits in this way:[20]

- Intelligence: Wide range of knowledge due to his well-rounded education. Keen sense of judgment. Very shrewd. Strong sense of bias.
- Libido: Strong sexual drive.
- Creativity: Strong imaginative power, which sometimes gets him into trouble.

---

[20] K.J. Sohn, *Kim Jong-il Report* (Seoul: Bada Publishing, 1993), pp.325, excerpt translated by John Cha

- Receptivity: He thinks big. But he has difficulty in accepting opposing views due to his inferiority complex, persecution complex.
- Adaptability: Rather than adapting to reality, he pursues constant change.
- Emotion: Always self-conscious about his image, popularity, and his artistic acumen.
- Ego: Underdeveloped ego makes him rely on authoritative means.
- Super Ego: His lack of self control leads him to be abrupt and reckless. Unable to establish his moral view.
- Internal conflict resolution: Rather than harmony he prefers extreme measures, aggressive action, i.e., hunting, shooting, self-punishment, driving, flying light airplanes.

A defector by the name of Kang Myong-do says that he had heard that Kim Jong-il slept with *Mein Kampf* by Adolf Hitler by his side. Professor Cho took his cue from this statement and did a comparative study between Hitler and Kim Jong-il.

Professor Cho claimed that first, both Hitler and Kim Jong-il had a strong desire for power. Secondly, he stated that neither was sympathetic toward humanity, although Kim Jong-il possessed better artistic sense. Thirdly, both of them lacked moral discipline, and their thought processes paralleled those of a young child. Professor Cho pointed to their respective family background, because neither of them had received attention when they were growing up. Hitler's father was a drunk and did not command his son's respect. Kim Jong-il, too, had problems with his father and his stepmother. Hitler and Kim both lost siblings early, affecting their psychological balance.

Finally, both of them were passionate about propaganda. It was important for Hitler to project his masculinity, as it was important for Kim Jong-il to project his masculinity, to the point of exaggeration.

They constantly monitored their colleagues and their political activities and enjoyed purging their traitors. In their struggle for power, they believed that they had to be crueler than their enemy and in the process felt satisfied that their enemies were well under control. Fifth, they had affinity for large-scale construction projects, great buildings and monuments, which can be explained as their way of compensating for their inferiority complex.

What can be concluded from these and other sources is that Kim Jong-il could be characterized as smart, quick-thinking, spontaneous, intuitive, humorous, and artistic. On the other hand, he was also competitive, jealous, and unable to deal with anyone more talented than him. He was narrow-minded, quick-tempered, and lacked the ability to control his emotions. He micro-managed and relied on his entrusted circle for policy decisions.

SECRECY

Secrecy means power, and Kim Jong-il was the master organizer of secrets. When he fell off a horse in 1992, he was laid up in a hospital for three months, but nobody knew what had happened to him or where he was, not even the members of the Party Central.

Kim Jong-il on a horse

Talking to former residents of North Korea, it is evident that they have been privy to little or no information about Kim Jong-il's personal life. They are shocked to learn where he was born, how many wives he had, his children, and his lifestyle. They quickly become disillusioned about the leader they once had adored and revered as they were growing up in the North. They grew up listening to his all-consuming rhetoric about his holy birthplace, his family lineage, and his accomplishments. They learn that much of it has been exaggerated, and the North Korean expatriates question everything about Kim Jong-il, beginning with his birth.

Was he truly born in the BaikDu Mountains?

Kim Jong-il believed he was. "When I was a child my mother told me many stories about BaikDu Mountains. She always told me that it was there that my father destroyed the Japanese imperialist robbers. She also told me that I was born there," he said in his official biography.

His father, Kim Il-sung, is quoted to say, "Whenever I see the BaikDu Mountains, I think of comrade Kim Jong-il. BaikDu is his hometown, the cradle of his being. His ideology and character emanate from there. It is amazing how he took after BaikDu in spirit, temperament, and every other way possible. He is the true son of BaikDu." Kim Il-sung further reinforces the significance of being born in the BaikDu Mountains in his memoirs:

> Apple trees bear apples and pear trees pears. That is the law of nature. Likewise, descendents of BaikDu are bound to be born with all the essence of BaikDu.

There have been endless stories about his birth, legends, and tributes surrounding his birth, but North Korean people in general do not hear about the fact that he was born in Habvrosk, Russia. They instead hear the legend:[21]

> A new star appeared at the BaikDu plateau in February at the height of wintry thunders and the thickest fog in the valley, when the fireball of the sun rose above the Jong Il Peak. The thunders ceased and the fog cleared while a grand rainbow stretched across the sky. A great boulder in the shape of a dragon horse flew down to the valley and lowered itself for a child dressed in armor.
>
> The child mounted it, held onto a rock in the shape of a saber, tapped the horse once, and rode up the rainbow. That night the sky was clear with the general's star so bright and the moon smiling nearby, a tiny new star in between.

The BaikDu legends continue in his official biography printed in Pyongyang: "From the moment he walked, he showed unusual brightness and ability to think, far ahead of his age...." and go on.

---

[21] Translated by John Cha, an excerpt from *General Kim Jong-il, Our Guiding Sun*, Hyangdo-ui Tae Yahng Kim Jong-il Jahng Goon, edited by Jang Seok, Ri Ju-cheol, Pyongyang Publishing, February 1995

As a kindergartener, he read newspapers and magazines and understood their meaning. He was very good in math and he could solve complex math problems with ease. In his elementary and middle school, he absorbed all the knowledge of the East and the West. He accompanied his father to farmlands and factories all across the country, where he learned about the value of labor and fostered his affection and respect for workers.

During the Korean War, he stood by his father, the commander-in-chief, and watched him score one victory after another. During his school years, he exhibited intellect and a passion for curiosity, the elements for his becoming an extraordinary thinker and capable politician.

The moment he entered the Korean Workers' Party and began working with the Central Committee, he demonstrated his leadership and organizational skills. One could tell that he was destined to lead and that he would live up to the promises his birth brought to Koreans.

Rhetoric of this type is excessive, in that it is hard to live up to the expectations that these words create, not to mention its inaccuracies, which harm Kim Jong-il's credibility over the long term, especially outside North Korea. North Korean expatriates become bitter and blame Kim Jong-il for all the ills that the country is suffering, mainly the shortage of food and energy. Kim Jong-il's penchant for super secrecy has not really served him well in the end. Kim Jong-il would have been better off presenting himself as a regular human being with his share of faults and quirks.

Kim understood the pitfalls associated with unceasing propaganda about himself. South Korean film director Sheen Sang-ok was at a party with Kim Jong-il, when about ten young female entertainers danced into the room singing in unison "Long live Comrade Dear Leader Kim Jong-il! *Mansei!*" and hopped up and down endlessly. Kim Jong-il grabbed Sheen's hand and shook it back and forth, saying, "Sheen *sunsaeng,* they're all fakes. They're lying." This incident, recorded by Sheen, indicates that Kim understood the reality of the exaggerated worship on the part of the public, or at least the young dancers at the party. Yet he allowed the practice to go on.

SECRET PARTIES

Kim Jong-il's secret party is the inner sanctum of the most powerful men in the land. It was Kim's version of the "smoke-filled back room." Many key decisions are made there, personnel matters in particular. The members of the elite ruling class meet regularly—by invitation only. Press reports describe these secret parties in an unflattering manner, i.e., a free-for-all drunken orgy and so on. This characterization appears to be exaggerated. Kim Jong-il started to hold secret parties in 1974—about the time he was named the successor, as a means to build a network among his close friends and colleagues. He invited his favorite stage artists and movie actors to join him and his friends at the gathering. Soon, the parties grew and included many VIPs from the Workers' Party, or the Party, military service, and various executive branches.

Korean culture in general demands considerable social interaction in work situations. Building mutual trust through friendship with their colleagues or the people they do business with is crucial among men and women (mostly men). They get together for dinner and drinking sessions. They throw down shot after shot, laugh and sing, all the time measuring each other and trying to get inside each other's mind and heart. The underlying philosophy is that a wise man knows that everlasting fellowship is more valuable than money or possessions. A true prince values honor, loyalty, devotion, and camaraderie. Pursuit of physical pleasure is not the driving motivation behind these parties, although they have been known to get out of hand now and then.

In the early 1970s, this secret party consisted of about twenty people, including Lee Yong-mu, the head political officer of the Defence Department, Kim Sung-yoon from the Security Bureau, mostly the younger party officials.

The number grew to about forty around 1977 and included Huh Dahm (former chairman of the Foreign Affairs Committee of the Party Central Committee); Kim Young-nam (current chairman of the Supreme People's Committee); Yeon Hyung-mook (former prime minister); Kim Yong-soon (former secretariat of the Party); Jang Song-thaek (Kim Jong-il's brother-in-law and current alternate member of the Political Bureau of the Party Central Committee, and vice chairman of the DPRK National Defence Commission); Rhee Myung-jae (former deputy director of Mansudan artists group); Choi Ik-gyu (current deputy director, Information Department); Choi Young-chol, Choi Chol-yong, and Ri Jay-gang (former deputy directors of the Organizational Department)—all of whom were frequent participants.

Generally, the party would take place at a building near Kim Jong-il's office every Wednesday and Saturday typically about eight in the evening. The participants called this space the "fish house" because of the huge aquarium, about nine feet high and twenty-four feet long, with large ocean fish swimming inside it. There is a swimming pool on the basement floor, game facilities on the first floor, as well as a mahjong room, a roulette room, and a restaurant. The participants would go up to the second floor, which was about 4,500 square feet with a stage to one side. At the entrance stood the "officer of the day" (participants took turns as the officer of the day) whose job was to greet the guests and give them each a glass of whisky.

When Kim Jong-il would sit down at the head table, which was closest to the stage, with four or so other guests around him, waiters would then bring out a variety of food—Korean, Chinese, Japanese, and Western. Kim Jong-il would make a toast, and the party would begin as the band started playing music. As the party wore on, Kim Jong-il would direct the people to sing. "So-and-so will sing now." South Korean songs were popular, and Kim Jong-il enjoyed singing "Wild Flower," "Teacher from Island Village," and "Farewell," and Russian songs like "Troika," and "A Night in Moscow." People danced the waltz and tango, joined by performing artists from the national dance troupe and theater groups. The party lasted till one in the morning, sometimes three, whenever Kim Jong-il became inebriated.

Kim Jong-il dispensed gifts once a month. Men received shoes or material for suits, and women received cosmetic sets or expensive Japanese lingerie. Once a year, Kim Jong-il prepared expensive gifts for the guests, including Rolex or Omega watches. On special occasions, he would hang two large balls, six feet in diameter, filled with myriad presents. When the party reached its peak, Kim Jong-il brought out his electronic gun and shot at the balls, which were equipped with an electric gate. The gates opened, and the presents poured down to the floor, and to his delight, his guests scrambled for the presents.

Sometimes, he would dole out an instant promotion and tell a person, "From now on, you're a member of the Party Central." Another time, he would tell a less fortunate person, "You're fired." One never knew what was in store for them at these parties. Yi Sang-tae, for instance, didn't know what to expect when he was invited to the party.

He had just been promoted to the position of deputy director of the Information Department, which put him on the list for the secret party. He was a literary critic by trade and edited the teachings of Kim Il-sung for the Party Central. He was appalled when he stepped into the fish house for the first time. He saw young women dancing in scant clothing and a group of men playing cards with dollar bills piled up in the middle of the table. Straight and narrow, he couldn't bring himself to join in the fun. He sat in the next room and smoked cigarettes until the end of the party, refusing to mix with the regulars. He was never invited to the party again. Yi didn't know that Kim Jong-il only trusted those who imbibed alcohol.

Kim Jong-il, connoisseur of wine

South Korean actress Choi Eun-hee often attended these parties, and she described this scene in the book she co-authored with her husband, Sheen Sang-ok:[22]

> Kim Jong-il called me out for a movie or a musical followed by a party almost every Friday. I came to know his sister and her husband as well. First time I met them was during dinner at the dining room in the Party Central building.
> At one point, he turned to me and said, "Choi *sunsaeng*, would you like to meet my sister?"

---

[22] Choi Eun-hee and Sheen Sang-ok, *I Am Kim Jong-il*, Nae Rae Kim Jong-il Ib-neh-da, (Seoul: Hang Lim Publishing, 1994)

I replied, "Yes." He turned around to his helpers behind him and said, "Call Kyoung-hui and tell her to come quick."

It was past one in the morning. Kim Kyoung-hui and her husband arrived about thirty minutes later. She stood about five feet two inches tall and looked healthy with her round face and plain-looking perm. She wore a chestnut colored two-piece suit. Her husband was tall, handsome, and refined. Kim Jong-il made introductions.

Kyoung-hui said, "Welcome. I am so glad you're here. Please stay healthy." Her husband smiled and said, "I am Jang Song-thaek."

After a few drinks, my handler Kim Hak-soon stood up and asked me to sing a song. I said I couldn't sing.

Someone said to Hak-soon, "You sing first." She sang and when she finished, she pointed to me to sing.

I stood up even though I had no idea what I should sing. She had taught me some songs praising Kim Il-sung, but I couldn't remember the words.

I stood hesitating, and Kim Jong-il said, "Choi *sunsaeng,* sing that song, you know the *Farewell* song by Patti Kim. Sing that one."

Everyone clapped. I was surprised that he knew the song from the South. In fact, he was very familiar with all the popular songs in the South. This song happened to be my favorite song as well. I started singing, "His heart is cold but he'll remember that night, his promise to me. He'd remember and regret that he left me over the hill far far away …"

I couldn't continue. I kept seeing Sang-ok through my tears. The band kept playing even though I stopped singing. Hak-soon thought I forgot the words to the song and recited the words for me. I barely managed to finish the song with her help.

Everyone clapped and hollered, "One more song!" I didn't know what to sing, Kim Jong-il said, "Sing *The Boarder Student.*"

I knew the melody, but the words escaped me. I stood there, trying to figure out how it began, when someone started, "Roaming is the way of life, where does it begin …"

107

Then I recalled the rest of the song. Then I went on to sing other songs, *Wheat Field, Boulder on the Hill,* and *Doraji* song.

Kim Jong-il was full of praise for me. "Your talent for singing matches your acting ability."

Kim Kyoung-hui and her husband Jang were next. They sang *Sunflower,* a song praising Kim Il-sung. After a while Kim Jong-il asked his sister, "Kyoung-hui, how about treating Choi sunsaeng a cup of tea at your place tonight?"

She replied, "Sure, that's fine."

It was already three in the morning. I got into a car with Kim Jong-il and Hak-soon and headed for Kyoung-hui's house. It was dark and I had no idea where we were going, but her home was inside the city limits. Her home was a modest one. We were served ginseng tea. I congratulated Kyoung-hui for having her second son as we drank tea.

Choi Eun-hee's experiences with the secret parties were uneventful other than dining on elaborate meals and singing songs late into the night. She did not mind these parties except for the few occasions when she was expected to drink with the group. She writes about one occasion when she was summoned at five in the morning.

When I arrived at the place I saw many dark colored Mercedes Benz's parked out in front. As I entered the front door, I was overwhelmed by the smell of liquor.

About forty to fifty people including a number of women I had never seen before were in the room. Obviously, they had been drinking all night long.

Kim Jong-il saw me and said, slurring his words, "Uh, Choi *sunsaeng,* you made it. Someone give her a drink."

Soon, several men offered me drinks all at once, hollering 'Bottoms up!' I took their glass and took a sip and quickly spat it out into a napkin when they weren't looking.

But some men wanted me to down the glass and stood watching, and I had to empty the glass. After a few glasses my head spun and I felt hot.

On the stage, a music band, women in their twenties, were playing songs Kim Jong-il requested. He kept changing his mind about which songs for them to play, even in the middle of songs, and the girls looked very tired.

He turned to me and asked me to conduct the band. I declined and his deputies, appalled at my refusal, urged me to conduct the band. "Comrade Choi, our Dear Leader only asks special people to conduct the band. It's an honor. You should do it."

So I stood up and pretend like I was a conductor.

"Wow. Wonderful! You're the best. When did you learn to conduct like that?" Kim hollered and clapped his hands and everyone followed suit. They forgot that I was an actress.

I felt tired and annoyed that I had to join the drinking session at dawn. They were having fun, but I certainly wasn't. The liquor got to me and I couldn't stay up any more. Kim saw me struggle and said to a woman seated next to him, "Let Choi *sunsaeng* rest a little."

The woman helped me up to a room upstairs. I sat on a sofa and leaned back with my eyes closed. I dozed off for a while and suddenly I felt someone's lips on my cheek. I sprang up and saw deputy communication minister Lim (he was the one who kidnapped me in Hong Kong) giggling like a fool.

I slapped his face as hard as I could and yelled, "How dare you do this!"

Startled, he said, "What's the big deal ..."

I cursed at him for a long time and went downstairs.

All in all, these party sessions were a well-kept secret, that was, until Rhee Myung-jae's wife got wind of the shenanigans that went on late into the morning. On party nights, her husband would come home drunk to the point of unconsciousness and pass out, muttering strange things in his sleep. A professor at the Kim Il-sung University, she wrote an anonymous letter to Kim Il-sung complaining about the goings-on at the party. "Our future comrade leader shouldn't engage in such untoward activities. This is a matter for Su Ryong-nim to sort out."

Her letter never reached Kim Il-sung. It was intercepted by the National Security Bureau and passed on to Kim Jong-il, who in turn ordered an investigation of all the attendants except Oh Jin-U, then the minister of defence.

She was caught after two months of grueling investigation. Kim Jong-il ordered an execution at the Security Bureau in Yong Sung

District. All the party attendants were there to witness the execution, including Rhee Myung-jae. Eager to show his loyalty to Kim Jong-il, Rhee volunteered to shoot his wife, and Kim Jong-il granted his permission.

Shooting your own wife is unthinkable under any circumstances, whether she had committed a capital crime or not. Apparently, Kim Jong-il thought and Rhee Myung-jae concurred that writing a letter to Kim Il-sung and complaining about the secret party was a serious offense punishable by death.

Several months later, Rhee remarried a woman introduced by none other than Kim Jong-il. Needless to say, no one since has dared to reveal the existence of a secret party or what went on there.

THE RHEE MYUNG-JAE INCIDENT AND ITS IDEOLOGICAL CONSEQUENCE

The Rhee Myung-jae incident is difficult to understand, but basically, we can see that loyalty to SuRyong's system has overriding priority over familial relationships. When you consider that North Korea is supposed to be founded on JuChe, whose first principle states that "human beings are the masters of all material things and thoughts that exist in the universe," Mrs. Rhee's execution does not speak well for the system.

Kim Jong-il wrote in his book, *Regarding JuChe*: "JuChe idea is the new, humanist philosophy ... Why must we see the world through the human's point of view? That is because humans, the most advanced beings of all the beings on earth, determine their own fate in this universe."

These words seem to indicate that Kim Jong-il placed high value in humanity. But then how do you leap from this humanistic treatise to the inhumane outcome that Rhee Myung-bae's wife faced? Was she an exception to the rule, or was Kim confused about what is human and what is not? He may have forgotten or never understood the original intent of the JuChe philosophy, perhaps.

The principle at work here is quite simple: what's good for Kim Jong-il is good for everyone. When you examine how the proletarian dictatorship concept evolved into the working model of Kim Il-sung-ism over the years, Rhee's action is not surprising. Glorification of the human spirit, the founding principle of JuChe philosophy, was transformed to glorification of Kim Il-sung and Kim Jong-il over the years.

What's interesting, Kim's words are remarkably similar to those of Hwang Jang-yop, who had authored several volumes of books on this very topic. Hwang held the identical anthropocentric point of view of the JuChe philosophy. Hwang spent most of his life contemplating and writing about the origin of life, the origin of man, evolution of man, thoughts of higher order, collectivism, individualism, and JuChe philosophy. Hwang was also Kim's mentor, which explains the similarities these men share.

Talking to Hwang, though, he was very bitter about what happened to the JuChe document that he had produced and was subsequently "edited" by Kim Jong-il. Kim took the liberty of revising the text without consulting Hwang, for reasons that "people would have difficulty in understanding all those philosophical terms," and so he simplified the language. In truth, Kim didn't understand the fundamentals of the anthropocentric philosophy, nor was he interested. According to Hwang, Kim only wanted the document to serve his own agenda, that is, to add legitimacy to his absolute power.

Mrs. Rhee believed in the purity of the JuChe system and was not aware of the real power behind it. She wrote the letter to Kim Il-sung believing that it would stop the untoward activities at Kim Jong-il's secret parties. She undoubtedly believed that the country operated under the true principles of revolution as spelled out in JuChe. But JuChe and its socialist utopia only turned out to be the front for Kim Il-sung-ism and his brand of Ten Commandments. There is a huge gap between the words of JuChe and proletarian dictatorship in action. Apparently, Mrs. Rhee didn't know or understand this when she took up her pen against Kim Jong-il.

Like Mrs. Rhee, the North Korean people seem to know very little about the inner workings of the Party. Interview after interview, I have found that former residents of the North know nothing about the private life of Kim Jong-il, how many wives he had, their names, their children, and so on. They become irate when they learn about Kim Jong-il's lifestyle, about his special resorts scattered around the best parts of the country, and how he indulged in the finest caviar, cheese, wine, and brandy from all over the world, not to mention his collection of cars.

Former northern residents echo, "I had no idea!" about his high living. A few elite core people did know, however, and once the word got out about the secret party, a rumor circulated that he was an alcoholic. The rumor wasn't entirely unfounded. There are many stories associated with his drinking binges.

Former diplomats describe the following incident that took place in Pyongyang in December 1987.[23]

> There was a convention in Pyongyang for all the foreign
> service officials, ambassadors and consuls who were
> dispatched around the world, to review the state of affairs
> in terms of their ideological education, progress reports on

---

[23] K.J. Sohn, *Kim Jong-il Report*, (Seoul: Bada Publishing, 2003), p. 386, excerpt translated by John Cha

carrying out the instructions issued by Kim Il-sung and Kim Jong-il, and discuss the plans for the upcoming year.

After a long month, Kim Jong-il held a banquet for the officials to show his gratitude for their hard work. It was a gala affair with many famous actresses among them, including Oh Miran.

Kim Jong-il appeared at seven in the evening. Usually, the guests would be seated in the hall first and, when he walked in, they would stand up and clap until he sat down.

This day, the opening reception was a bit different from the usual routine. Kim Jong-il, Kim Young-nam the Minister of Foreign Affairs, Kang Seok-ju the First Deputy Minister and other deputies were already there inside the hall.

The ambassadors were called out one at a time according to their ranks, to be greeted by Kim Jong-il, and the others surrounding him, along with a full glass of French cognac. The diplomats were required to drink the cognac "bottom up," which was the price of admission.

They picked up the glass and saluted to Kim Jong-il, "Long live comrade dear leader."

Kim Jong-il clanked his bowl-shaped glass and replied, "Thank you."

Then the diplomat downed the full glass (size of a mug) in one gulp. By the time the ninety or so diplomats made their entrance this way, some older diplomats already were sprawled over tables, passed out.

Kim Jong-il shot them a disgusted look and said, "They can't drink at all. And they call themselves men." He left the banquet shortly afterwards. His parting words were, "The night is on me. Eat and drink to your heart's content. I brought actresses, too, so dance hardy. I'll be going now. Minister Kim, make sure they have a good time."

Kim Jong-il, as a matter of habit, didn't stay around long for any official event. Being a private person, he preferred to do business at his secret parties with his close, loyal colleagues. Whatever he said at these parties was recorded and deemed as official instructions for the party organization and its members to follow.

Here's an account by a woman who was at these secret parties. She goes by the name Mi-hyang and recently talked about her past association with Kim Jong-il. She defected to the South in 1998 following her luxurious life in Kim Jong-il's inner circle. [24]

> When I saw Kim Jong-il on television recently and how weak he looked, I realized that life was truly empty. What I know about him is not a matter of national security or anything important like that. I really don't see what good my story would do.
>
> Everything is going to come out when he dies, anyway. I'm not sure whether I should talk about this or not. It already has been twelve years since I saw him last.
>
> It all began when I was drafted by Section 5 of the Party central. The Party officials go around all the schools in the country and select pretty girls as candidates to serve in Section 5. This selection process is rigorous and it takes about a year to complete. They examine appearance, character, devotion and loyalty, voice, height, virginity, and all the tests you could think of. They selected ten finalists, and I was one of them.
>
> After I concluded all the tests during that year, a car came to my house one night. A Party official came inside and presented my parents with a plaque containing words of thanks for raising a capable child who is chosen to serve the fatherland in a special way. He also gave my parents a huge sum of money.
>
> They took me to a secret school after I signed my pledge of loyalty. This pledge includes writing in my blood. I cut my thumb with a sharp knife they gave me until it bled. I wrote, "I pledge my loyalty."
>
> After the pledge, they drove me in a Mercedes Benz, its windows covered with curtains. I couldn't see outside or the driver. I only knew that the school was located in a secluded place outside Pyongyang. The school building was in the shape of a half moon, three stories above and below ground level. Kim Jong-il's statue stood in the middle of the school. It was a military school.
>
> When I got there first, I stayed in a room with hardly anything in it. Bathroom and blankets, that was all. There

---

[24] Chu Sung-ha, "The Mi-hyang Story," DongA.com, February 2, 2010

was a small window, but it was too high for me to look out. At night I heard strange sounds and I was scared. A man brought my meals, which was the only time I saw anyone. I couldn't speak to him. He also brought books every day, books I had seen outside, about Kim Il-sung, Kim Jong-il, history of revolution, as well as novels. I had to read the books and write a report.

Sometimes, I had to write a variety of reports on one particular book and I had a hard time doing it. I could have piled up these books and stand on them to look out the window, but I didn't dare because of the closed circuit television cameras that seemed to follow me around. It was just like a prison. I was confused and anxious about my situation.

Fortunately, my meals had an interesting variety, international cuisine, and I relaxed somewhat. I thought that it wasn't a prison, after all. I lived like this for a month.

Then I got to meet the rest of the ten girls. They all were very pretty, and a foreign looking girl was there, too. I seemed to be the youngest, but nobody knew how old everyone was. We weren't allowed to have private conversations. We were told that we were starting school and given military uniform with a necktie as part of initiation.

My life changed. First, I was allowed to go outside, including outings to Pyongyang once or twice a week. We got to dress up and go to nice places and fine restaurants. We ate in a private room at Hyang Man Ru, a fancy restaurant.

They took tons of pictures, with or without makeup. We studied and trained in all kinds of subjects. We trained in shooting, swimming, arts, and etiquette. Three women taught us.

Sometimes we played games. We played this computer game called, "Protect the General." When you get rid of all the enemies, a curly haired man dressed in a jumper suit comes out and claps and waves his hand. It's Kim Jong-il.

I moved into a new place with Mi-ok. She was one of the instructors and her rank was a colonel. But she didn't wear a uniform. We were so much alike, same height, same looks, and we could pass for sisters. She looked after me, and she always was with me when I saw Kim Jong-il. There was another girl named Young-mi who majored in opera in Ham Heung Art School. She lived with Mi-so, another instructor.

One summer day in 1995, about six months into the school, Mi-ok called for Young-mi and me and told us in a serious tone in her voice, "You have been selected to assist General Kim Jong-il."

She instructed us about how to conduct ourselves in front of Kim Jong-il. For instance, we were to behave calm and cool, never to over react to what he said. "Just watch me and clap when I do."

I didn't sleep that night. I was treated like a queen from that day on. Hairdressers, tailors, and massage therapists came and went, and even make-up people. The day came when I was to meet the general. They gave me a new dress to wear and gave me light makeup.

Mi-ok and I rode a car with curtains around its windows. When we arrived at his place, Mi-so and Young-mi were there along with another girl. Mi-ok went inside first and came back out. She signaled to follow her inside and we did. Seeing him, I felt the urge to yell out *mansei,* as I was taught to do all my life, but I remembered Mi-ok's warning about being calm and cool. I held myself back and watched what Mi-ok did. She casually shook hands with Kim Jong-il, and I did the same. We sat at a table, and Mi-ok introduced me to Kim Jong-il. He wanted me to introduce myself as well, and I did. I shook all over.

We had Italian food, steak, spaghetti, and wine. Shark's fin dish, too. It was the best meal I ever had. I was very tense and I just kept my head down and focused on the food. Mi-ok and Mi-so looked comfortable chatting with him, though. Kim Jong-il told me, "Relax and enjoy your food."

He tried to make me feel comfortable and he seemed like an *ajocee* from my old neighborhood, in an avuncular sort of way. He looked quite different from his pictures or images on television. He appeared pale and down at first but he improved as time went on. I noticed that his face had many dark spots and his teeth were yellow, contrary to my prior image of him as a perfect, god-like persona.

He treated us very well, though. He gave us presents, chocolates, Chinese moon cakes, and a wristwatch with his signature stenciled on its backside. He gave us pearl necklaces and cosmetics. We became familiar with each other to the point that he would pass gas without giving a second thought. He was very careful about that in the beginning.

He liked to hear us sing. Young-mi had a great voice since she had majored in opera singing. The first song she sang in front of Kim Jong-il was an aria entitled, "Don't Walk on the Cold Snow, General." [It is a song to pledge loyalty to Kim Jong-il and it goes something like, I pledge myself to the General, lest he walk in icy rainstorm, to give him joy every day, General, General, please be well.]

When Young-mi sang the part, "General, General" she wept profusely, full of emotion. I was thinking that she was doing great despite her exaggerated emotion that opera singers tend to express. I was expecting that Kim Jong-il would be moved by her singing, but he didn't seem very impressed. He simply said, "Well done. Nice voice."

It was my turn to sing next. I can't sing as well as Young-mi, and I was worried. I sang a Japanese song called "Mitsizure." Mi-ok had told me that it was his favorite song. I sang it in Japanese and Korean. [It goes something like, I told the duckweed floating in the pond about my lonely night, it looked at me with tears in its eyes, and nodded quietly, we are in the same boat, you are my companion.]

He told me that my singing and movement were very natural and asked me to sing another song. I sang "Subaru" for him. He said that "Mitsizure" was a better song for me.

Mi-ok asked him to sing a song, clapping her hands in rhythm. We joined her and clapped our hands yelling, "General, General."

Beaming a wide smile, he stood up and sang a Russian song. Mi-ok told me that it was a famous Russian song. As a singer, I thought he was alright, but not very good. He liked to dance to the blues, so we practiced dancing to the music. He didn't tell anyone about us. When we saw him, four of us were there alone with him except for rare occasions. He never got drunk with us. I heard that he sometimes got drunk and unruly. Once he was totally drunk and his assistant tried to tell him he'd had enough.

Kim Jong-il screamed and yelled, "Throw him in jail," and they did. Next morning when he looked for his assistant, they told him what happened. He didn't remember anything at all. He behaved like a gentleman when he drank with us. Sometimes he cried when we sang sad songs.

We ate well. I liked sushi the best, thin slices of fish wrapped over rice. Kim Jong-il loved sushi also. Shark's fin dish always was on the menu. Once he recommended a piece of shark meat, and I took a bite.

He smiled and asked, "Do you know what you're eating?"

I shook my head and replied, "I don't know."

Then he said it was shark's sex organ, and I almost threw up. He laughed really hard.

I think it was during our first meeting, when he asked me what my favorite food was. I told him that I liked *naeng myun* [cold noodles] the best. "I can eat it three times a day."

He said, "My father was like you. He liked *naeng myun* very much. But I'm not that crazy about it."

We went all over the place, countryside resorts and hunting resorts. We usually went ahead and waited for him. He hated people talking about his hidden resorts. There was one resort that sticks in my mind. It took about 40 minutes to get there by car through a tunnel. Everything was underground, an entertainment area, a swimming pool, bedrooms, and a restaurant. We swam in the luxurious pool with its bottom decorated with the Kim Jong-il flower [Kimjongilia].

This underground facility actually was more like a hideout than a resort. There are a number of them, underneath the Gwang Bok department store and schools. They're well insulated, so people have no idea they exist.

At the hunting grounds only Kim Jong-il carried a gun. Even Mi-ok didn't carry a gun. We trained in target shooting, but never in front of Kim Jong-il. He is an excellent shot. After the hunt the chef made delicious dishes with the pheasants he'd shot. The first time we went hunting, Kim Jong-il gave me a new name, Mi-hyang, meaning beautiful and captivating.

He would get confused with our names, Mi-ok, Mi-so, Mi-hyang, and Young-mi, which he later changed to Mi-ae. When he was drunk, he'd point at me and say, "You are Mi-ok? Mi-hyang? Ah, you're Mi-hyang." And he would repeat this after a while. Sometimes he'd ask, "Do you know what Ok means? It means she has jade-like skin."

Mi-ok was Kim Jong-il's secretary as well as his lover. She told me a lot of things and regarded me as her successor.

She'd hug me close and say, "You'll take over my duties some day. You and I must lead a lonely life." She was so sad whenever she said this to me. She was so nice. I called her comrade Mi-ok in public, but she had me call her *onni* when we were alone.

Generally, we're discharged from our service when we turn 26 or 27, at the rank of lieutenant or captain. But I'm pretty certain that Mi-ok will continue to serve Kim Jong-il because of their close relationship.

Other girls will be married off to his bodyguards so as to keep his secrets in-house. He had an interesting taste for women. He considered eyes as most important. He liked my black hair and black pupils. He thought that brown pupils went with brown hair. Then he looked at lips. He liked thick lips and a pronounced nose. He is very picky. He doesn't like heavy make-up. Once I showed up with long eyelashes, and he didn't like them at all. I never wore them again. He showed us how to spray perfume. "Spray them in the air and you walk into the mist." We exclusively used French cosmetics. We never wore heels taller than two inches. He didn't like women taller than he was.

Health

Kim Jong-il had always been known to be very healthy, almost legendarily. For years, he had been on the heavy side for his height, but with his team of doctors constantly looking after him, he remained in excellent shape until he reportedly suffered a stroke along with other ailments such as pancreatic cancer. He appeared weakened, amid all the speculations about his state of health and in the absence of any real information.

He had managed to pull through somehow, and the experts attributed his recovery to his healthy constitution.

According to Lee Young-kuk, former bodyguard, "Kim Jong-il was very healthy. He looked chubby on the outside, but when he climbed up Jong Dong Mountain in Pyongyang, or when he climbed stairs for two to three miles, he walked so fast, nobody could keep up with him. On many occasions, he would run by himself. He also swam more than ten laps in his pool, 120 meters long."

He ate the best food available. According to Lee Han-young, Sung Hye-rim's nephew, Kim Jong-il's rice was made of "moon duk" rice. Kim's chefs would go through each grain of rice and make sure they were whole, no cracks in them, before they were allowed to be cooked. Special wood was brought in from BaikDu Mountains to cook the rice. His kitchen staff made sure that each item was special for Kim Jong-il. He even had a special line for him at Ryong Sung beer brewery, and his staff monitored the line to ascertain the highest quality. His staff sent lists requesting foodstuffs to various embassies around the world, e.g., Portuguese tangerines; leg of lamb from Pakistan; melon and grapes from Shin Jang, China; bear's feet and goat's meat, eel, caviar, and other rare goods from Russia.

Kenji Fujimoto, Kim Jong-il's chef of thirteen years, talks about ten thousand bottles of liquor in his palace. He describes his special palm shark's fin soup (palm fruit carved to serve the shark fin soup) which he served for Russian and Chinese VIPs along with special caviar, coya (barbequed piglet), roasted fish on flat pan, sautéed pigeon in soy sauce, barbecued goat Russian style, *la clet* (French cheese on potato and eggplant), sautéed turtle fish …

To continue my refrain that most people I talked to know nothing of the luxurious life that Kim was leading, much less the kind of food he ate, they have only heard what the Information Department has told them: "Our comrade general always remembers the anti-Japan days and eats a ball of rice along with bean sprout soup and frozen tofu."

A young defector I recently interviewed said that she had taken part in the welcoming ceremony in Pyongyang for the Chinese premier Hu Jintao's visit in 2007. She and her friends noticed how Premier Hu looked so young and healthy compared to Kim Jong-il, even though they were the same age. She said that everyone lamented, "Our great general looks worse than Premier Hu because we didn't take care of our great general as well as we should have."

Kim Jong-il with Hu Jintao

Many North Korean people like this woman have turned inward and blamed themselves for Kim's unhealthy appearance. Their devotion to Kim Jong-il was remarkable. She and her friends should not have blamed themselves for Kim Jong-il's physical appearance at his meeting with Hu Jintao.

She couldn't have known that a German surgeon had performed heart bypass surgery on Kim in May 2007. She didn't know that Long Life Research Center was responsible for Kim's health; that the center had a team of specialists looking after his organs, such as heart specialists, liver specialists, and pancreas specialists, who were constantly monitoring him. The center had a group of people who have similar physical characteristics as Kim Jong-il, anatomical duplicates. When he needed a medical treatment, his medical staff tried the treatment methods on these people and ascertained the results. For example, if

Kim Jong-il's pancreas was an issue, they would find people with a similar problem and experiment with various treatments on them until the doctors found the right method.

Whatever his medical team did, Kim Jong-il seemed to have recovered from his ailments, as was seen by his meeting with former US president Bill Clinton in September 2009, when he was in Pyongyang to negotiate a release for two American journalists who allegedly had crossed the border without permission. The North Korean Information Department used Clinton's visit as a photo-op to show Kim's recovery of his health. Kim's visit to China in May 2010 provided another photo-op to show that his health was not a problem.

However, he appeared weak and scrawny, and physicians observed that he "dragged his left leg" as he walked from one place to another, while his left hand was immobile, not to mention his noticeable hair loss. No one was sure how long he would keep his health, but his physical condition prompted a crucial discussion about succession of power.

CHAPTER 9
DYNASTIC TRANSFER OF POWER

———

THE SUCCESSION QUESTION

September 28, 2010

All the speculations about whom Kim Jong-il would designate as his successor were over on September 28, 2010. That one of his three sons would be chosen to reign over the countless palaces strewn across the country was never in doubt. There was much discussion centered on which one would be tapped to do the honor. It was reported that Kim Jong-il's third son, Kim Jong-un (mothered by Ko Young-hee) was slated to become the next leader of the Party. For months, schoolchildren in Pyongyang had been seen marching through the streets singing a song called "Footsteps," praising "the young revolutionary soldier from the BaikDu family."

Other than the song, there had been no specific, detailed information about young Jong-un, beyond the fact that he was twenty-six or twenty-seven years old. According to the pictures published in *Rodong Sinmun,* the official newspaper of the Workers' Party, he is a carbon copy of his grandfather, Kim Il-sung, in physical appearance. His personality is said to be very similar to his father's. He has worked at the organizational department of the Party Central, which is involved in the personnel matters of the Party, just as his father had done at about the same age. He appears destined to follow his father's path to power, since he was promoted to a four-star general and was made the official successor at the Workers' Party convention on September 28, 2010.

Kim Jong-nam, his first son and previous heir apparent, supposedly fell out of favor when he was caught in Japan with a fake Dominican Republic passport in 2001. He publicly said that he was there to visit Disneyland in Tokyo. A veteran international traveler, he shouldn't have allowed himself and his companions, his wife, his son, and a helper, to get caught in this awkward position, attracting attention from the international press. Because of this incident, he was perceived as incompetent and relegated to roaming about in China, Macao, Hong Kong, and Russia.

Before this incident, he was the prince-in-waiting, heir apparent to succeed power from his father. Jong-nam grew up hearing his father say things like, "When you grow up, you will sit in this chair," or "You need to learn about economy if you are going to lead our nation." His father had left no doubt that Jong-nam would be the one to run the country when the time came. However, in a June 2009 interview with Japanese television, Jong-nam announced that he was not interested in politics and that his father favored Jong-un, the younger of his two half-brothers.

There also had been talk about Jong-chol, the older brother of Jong-un, as well. Their mother, Ko Young-hee, had tried to install Jong-chol as the successor, and for a period he was considered as one who could inherit the throne. Whether it was Jong-chol or Jong-un, Ko Young-hee strongly felt that one of her sons had to succeed to power, because that was the only way to preserve the lives of her sons. She was gravely concerned that her sons would fall victim to a vicious purge should Jong-nam take office. However, her attempt to propel Jong-chol into the forefront didn't work. Kim Jong-il declared, "No, he's too effeminate," and that was the end of Jong-chol's bid for power.

Her initiative at the least helped unseat Jong-nam as the heir apparent. For years she labored to create a distance between Jong-nam and his father, perhaps convincing Kim Jong-il to send Jong-nam to Switzerland for his schooling. When Jong-nam first went to Geneva in 1980 at the age of nine to attend elementary school, Kim Jong-il called Jong-nam every day, and they cried together on the telephone.

But Kim Jong-il's affection shifted to Jong-chol when he was born in 1981, followed by Jong-un in 1983, which left Jong-nam on his own in Geneva with his caretakers. Jong-nam returned to Pyongyang at the age of eighteen, and by that time, he was almost forgotten in the Kim household. His father was very disappointed about his lackluster performance as a student in Europe. As a teenager, Jong-nam had spent much of his time riding motorcycles and chasing girls instead of focusing on his studies.

He continued his cavorting ways when he returned to Pyongyang, partying extensively with his friends, which didn't sit well with his father either. There were other similar incidents that further annoyed his father, and their relationship deteriorated worse than ever. Then in 1996, his aunt Hye-rang defected, which caused tremendous hardships for Jong-nam, his mother, and his grandmother.

Dark clouds hung over the future of the three of them. Kim Jong-il would have felt betrayed by Hye-rang's action, and there was no predicting how he would react. Hye-rang's son, Lee Han-young, had already defected to the South some years before and had even written a book entitled *Kim Jong-il's Royal Family,* exposing details about Kim's private life, including where he lived, where he worked, and more.

As it turned out, his aunt's defection presented Jong-nam an opportunity to make amends with his father. He went to Kim Jong-il and expressed his regret over his aunt's defection, pointing out carefully that his mother was still loyal to the Party, and that so was he. Kim Jong-il was philosophical about the incident and assured Jong-nam that as long as he was loyal, everything was fine. Jong-nam pledged his undying loyalty to his father, and they became father and son once again. Not too long afterward, Lee Han-young was shot and killed by two gunmen in Bundang near his apartment.

By 1998, Jong-nam had fully recovered his status as the heir and was elected as a member of the Supreme People's Assembly. His linguistic ability (English, French, Chinese, Japanese, and Korean) led him to perform important functions for the Party, especially with regards to the IT industry and international trade. He traveled to Beijing, Macao, Hong Kong, Tokyo, and other cities for various business purposes, which were rumored to be related to weapons and drugs. When he was caught with a fake passport in Japan in 2001, he said that he and his family were there to visit Disneyland, but the Japanese officials knew better. Their investigation revealed that Jong-nam was in Japan to collect payment on a multinational deal concerning weapons shipment. By this time, he was in charge of Office 39, which is responsible for the international trade business for the Party.

This passport mishap placed him in an awkward position, and rumors persisted that he wasn't allowed to go back to Pyongyang. There is no way of knowing exactly what transpired between Jong-nam and his father. They wouldn't talk, and true to ruling leadership's usual modus operandi, they mask what really happened and keep the rest of the world guessing. Studying his TV interviews in Beijing and Macao, Jong-nam actually appeared amused about the pesky press that kept hounding him. He didn't seem annoyed by all the attention and seemed to enjoy the cat-and-mouse game with the press crew. He is even said to have hired a lookalike to masquerade as a decoy.

In the midst of all this, Ko Young-hee was busy grooming her sons, Jong-chol and Jong-un, trying to ensure that one of them became the designated leader. After their elementary schooling in Berne, Switzerland, they entered the Kim Il-sung Military Academy to learn about military theories and strategy. Kim Jong-il also went along with the idea to present Ko Young-hee to the nation as "the nation's mother" to legitimize her status and therefore Jong-chol and Jong-un's status.

Ko Young-hee, mother of Jong-chol and Jong-un

Ko Young-hee's naming as "nation's mother" came about after her sister, Ko Young-sook, and her husband, Pak Gun, in Berne defected to the United States in 1998. Ko Young-sook's defection dampened Ko Young-hee's drive to install one of her sons to succeed her husband. She did persist, however, in becoming more active in the nation's affairs. She accompanied Kim Jong-il on his tours of the military bases and discussed the succession matter with him. By the time Sung Hye-rim, Jong-nam's mother, died alone in Moscow in 2002, Ko Young-hee managed to keep an upper hand, and the Chinese and Japanese newspapers began reporting that Jong-chol had received the nod for succession.

Nothing was set in stone, though. Ko Young-hee died of breast cancer in 2004, not knowing if Jong-chol had been designated as the crown prince. As of December 2009, Jong-un appeared to be the forerunner in this race. In the meantime, Jong-nam judiciously said in his interview, "It is up to my father."

The struggle seemed to continue, and some even suspected that violence could be in the making. In June 2009, KBS (Korea Broadcast System) reported an assassination attempt on Jong-nam by Jong-un's supporters, during which Chinese authorities intervened on behalf of Jong-nam. Everyone, including the NIS (National Intelligence Service) of South Korea, denied the incident ever happened. Reporters caught up to Jong-nam in Beijing and asked him whether the assassination attempt was true. He ridiculed the notion: "Would I be running around like this if it was true?"

He denied the report, but the story left an impression that the Chinese favored Jong-nam over the others. Hwang Jang-yop agreed, "The Chinese stand behind Jong-nam because he would carry out the Chinese style of economic reform." A government-operated Chinese newspaper suggested that Jong-nam remained in the picture as a viable candidate because of his political acumen and his knowledge and expertise in international affairs as well as the computer industry. He was in charge of managing the Party's funds relative to the Chinese trade, which is an important consideration. They also point to the Confucian tradition of favoring the oldest son, which is rooted deep in the Korean culture.

Prominent in the picture is the presence of Kim Ok, Kim Jong-il's fourth wife. Kim Ok, twenty-two years younger than Kim Jong-il, was introduced to Kim Jong-il by Ko Young-hee before she died. Kim Ok majored in piano at Pyongyang Music and Dance School. Unlike

Sung Hye-rim or Ko Young-hee, she went beyond the simple role of a wife and was active in the affairs of the state. She accompanied Jo Myung-rok (1928-2010), former first deputy chairman of the Defence Commission, to the United States in October 2000. She was with Kim Jong-il when she met Hyundai's chairperson, Hyun Jung-eun, in July 2005. She accompanied Kim Jong-il to China in January 2006 and met with Premier Hu Jintao. Of all the women associated with Kim Jong-il, she has been the only one actively involved in the state affairs.

Kim Ok is known to support Jong-un, who is much younger than she, and it is thought that she would feel much more comfortable exercising her influence over him. Jong-nam, on the other hand, would present a control problem for her because he is only four years younger than she. In addition, Jong-nam has developed a long list of friends and cronies over the years, including heavyweights like Jang Song-thaek and his aunt Kim Kyoung-hui, who would all be difficult for Kim Ok to deal with and control.

For Jong-un to succeed, he would need to win the approval of the current ruling class by guaranteeing them a secure future. But he was far from being in a position to deliver such a guarantee. Instead, he was said to be causing fear among the ruling class because no one was sure who would become his target for purging.

A group called North Korean Intellectuals Solidarity predicted chaos the moment Kim Jong-il died. They believed that Jong-un and his supporters would make a move against Jong-nam, and Jong-nam's supporters would resist.

Hwang did not feel that a bloody confrontation was imminent even if Kim Jong-il died. He said in April 2010 that the situation would remain stable as long as Kim Kyoung-hui, Kim Jong-il's sister, and her husband, Jang Song-thaek, were around to manage the Party and the military. Jang was appointed deputy chairman of the Defence Commission of the Party, second only to Kim Jong-il. His brothers, Jang Sung-wu and Jang Sung-gill, command the troops stationed near Pyongyang. Jang, a participant in numerous purges in the past, is very familiar with the process of power transfer in Pyongyang.

FOUR POSSIBLE SCENARIOS FOR THE KIM DYNASTY

Nothing is certain when it comes to a power play in Pyongyang. Historically, Kim Jong-il has always managed come out on top, so chances are, he would get his way in prolonging the Kim dynasty. But he faced serious hurdles.

The most serious was his health. He had no idea how much time he had left in securing his dynastic dream. He needed a lot of time, ten years, to train his young son in the art of totalitarian dictatorship and to convince the Party cadres that Jong-un will take good care of them.

His second hurdle was that the North Korean people saw Kim Jong-il's rule as a failure because of the massive famine that claimed 3 million lives. Third, the economy worsened due to the failed currency reform.

According to North Korea watchers, Kim Jong-un is not going to have an easy time succeeding his father as the next leader. A twenty-seven-year-old, he does not have the experience, they say, nor does he have enough support among the Party elites to become the leader his father had hoped. At present, the Party propaganda machine is busy promoting him as "Kim Jong-un, the young, brilliant commander" with superior knowledge in military matters. The Party continues to paint him as a military genius, and the public most likely will accept him as such.

Still, many things could happen, K.J. Sohn says, and he worked out four different scenarios for the transfer of power and presented them at a seminar in London in 2011, before Kim Jong-il passed.

Scenario 1: Dynastic succession

In this scenario, Kim Jong-un secures his positions in the Party, the military, and the Executive Department, followed by a period of father-son joint rule. During this period, the son carries out the father's instructions. The son eventually takes over and goes solo after a number of years. This scenario is very similar to Kim Jong-il's succession from Kim Il-sung in 1974.

Kim Jong-un will vie for and secure various key positions, including a membership in the Central Committee of the Workers' Party Political

Bureau (Party Central); and positions as deputy chairman of the Organizational Department of the Secretary Bureau, deputy chairman of the Military Committee of the WPK, etc.

Kim Jong-il will facilitate the securing of these positions for Jong-un and will order the Party elites, the army personnel, the police department, and other departments to pledge their loyalty to Jong-un. This scenario would be an extension of the Kim Il-sung/Kim Jong-il era, which means that the military-first policy would continue with little change in the nuclear weapons strategy.

In the short term, it is anticipated that the power structure will be able to sustain itself. But as time goes on, especially after Kim Jong-il's death, there is a strong possibility that conflicts would arise between the old and the new power elites. Similar conflicts existed between the old and the new elites following Kim Il-sung's death, which led to the wholesale purge called *Shim Hwa Jo*.

Scenario 2: Guardianship

This scenario is a "modified third-generation succession" scheme in the event that Kim Jong-il suddenly dies. In this case, Jang Song-thaek takes on the duty of a guardian for Jong-un. Together, they will continue to assign important positions to close associates of Kim Jong-il and other elites.

As time goes on, however, it is very possible that there will be differences in opinion between Kim Jong-un and Jang. This could result in a conflict between Jang's faction and supporters of Kim Jong-un. There is the potential for power struggle on the part of the elites from the Party, the military, or the Security Bureau.

Scenario 3: Collective leadership

Some experts predict that the elites from the Political Bureau of the Party and the National Defence Commission would propose a collective leadership structure. In reality, however, the possibility for this scenario to occur is very low. North Korea has never experienced group leadership during the Kim Il-sung/Kim Jong-il era, and it would be difficult to introduce a collective system of rule. There is no clear reason for Kim Jong-un or Jang to revive the Political Bureau of the Party. There is even less reason to revive the antiquated institutions like the party convention that are no longer effective.

Some people, outside the power circle, would also demand a collective leadership structure, but there is no instrument to effect this demand. Some elites could join forces with an ambitious faction within the military and attempt a coup d'état, but chances of success for this scheme are very remote also.

Scenario 4: Long-term power instability

In the event that Kim Jong-il suddenly died without defining the procedure for the power transfer, or Jang failed to secure the powerbase for over a year after Kim Jong-il's death, the North Korean society will face destabilization. In this scenario, it is highly likely that an internal power struggle would erupt. If the situation persists, powerful military members could gain power, or there could be a state of anarchy. A state of anarchy mostly likely would prompt mass exodus of the people.

Of all these scenarios, Kim Jong-il would prefer the first scenario, in which the power is successfully transferred to his son, just as his father had done for him. Every father in the world would like to pass on his legacy to his son, wouldn't they? Jong-un's case is different. When Kim Jong-il succeeded Kim Il-sung, there was a ten-year period from 1974 to 1985 when there was father-son joint leadership. Kim Jong-il began to gain authority in all areas, and then after 1985, he began to rule the country. The Kim Il-sung regime changed step by step to the Kim Il-sung/Kim Jong-il joint leadership regime.

In order to achieve a similar result, Kim Jong-un needs to have the following conditions:

(1) Kim Jong-il's health to remain stable for about ten years;
(2) prevention of internal fighting over the succession issue;
(3) stable internal and external environment economically and politically.

Given his father's sudden death, however, Jong-un does not have the luxury of a ten-year transition program. Without an adequate amount of time, the succession scheme would result in a temporary regime or fail altogether.

During the second succession in 1974, the economic and political situation were stable, allowing for Kim Jong-il to play out his bid for the top job. Kim Jong-il also had the support of the original partisans, while Jong-un has not had an opportunity to build his own support base.

CORRUPTION OF POWER

I once asked a US congressman why he stayed in the House of Representatives for twenty-four years. "Running for office every two years is a lot of work; campaigning, fundraising, the stress of it all. What drives you?"

I asked him to be honest, and he replied, "Power is like drugs. Once you taste it, you can't let it go."

So refreshing and candid, I thought, and thanked him for his answer, wishing that more politicians were honest like him. I had expected a pat answer like, "I want to serve the people," or "I want to pay back for all that I received from the community," something along that line. But I was wrong to presume that he would feed me the usual self-serving rhetoric.

I always thought that, if I ever got a chance to meet Kim Jong-il, I would have liked to ask him the same question: what drives you to stay in power? I wonder if he would have given me a straight answer. I can imagine his answer to be something like, "My mother. She told me that it was my destiny to lead the Korean people," or "I'm doing it for my son. I want to leave behind a decent republic for him to manage." I can empathize with this sort of answer, for it would jibe with the truthful side of his personality.

Or he could have given me the official party line version: "I'm building a paradise on earth, for my love of humanity. I am here to repel imperialist invaders and reunite all of Korea."

Well, this sort of rhetoric may resonate with the North Korean public, as it has for many years, but it wouldn't work in, say, California. Nevertheless, the hoi polloi of North Korea are also having a change of heart. Ever since the food rationing system went awry, the people put less stock in the "paradise on earth." During the famine in 1997 and 1998, people were told to hang on; the "arduous march" would not last forever, and the food rationing system would be reinstated soon.

People trusted the officials and waited for the better times to return. Many died waiting. Recognizing that "life in the paradise on earth" should not include starvation, the people of North Korea are no different from anyone else on earth. They want food on a regular basis, preferably three meals a day, education for their children, and medical service. Their government was supposed to provide these services for free. Instead of dispensing food, the Party officials have continuously espoused the "arduous march."

Needless to say, the usual rhetoric has lost its meaning as time has passed. Finally the Party announced that the people should fend for themselves, on their own, and even allowed for the people to buy and sell rice in makeshift marketplaces. Markets sprung up across cities and villages (six hundred to two thousand locations) for people to trade rice, vegetables, eggs, corn, and other grains. People then relied on the marketplace for their daily needs.

People have now gotten used to fending for themselves and see little use for the Party and its policies. If there was any doubt about the incompetency of the Party policies, the latest debacle, the so-called currency reform, took care of that.

On November 30, 2009, the Party Central carried out a currency reform designed to regain control over the nation's economy, which was "getting out of hand" because of the burgeoning markets. The markets were creating a bourgeois class, even wealthy merchants, against all socialist principles. The government issued new money and gave everyone one week to exchange the old money for the new. They also set a limit on the amount of old money that could be exchanged: 100,000 won per family ($735). In other words, people could exchange only a portion of the old money. What happened to the rest of the old money? It became worthless paper.

As a result, people lost their life savings, and they openly exhibited their dissatisfaction. There were reports of graffiti denouncing Kim Jong-il and open hostilities toward police officers and local party officials. Such overt demonstration against Kim Jong-il and the party elites was an alarming development, and the Party Central decided to pacify the masses by issuing an open apology and increased the exchange limit to three hundred thousand won.

They also blamed the failed currency reform on Park Nam-ki (minister of planning and finance) and executed him in public. Park's execution may have silenced the public, but it didn't solve the basic problem. Inflation skyrocketed, increasing upward ten to twenty times. The price of rice hit the roof, about $110 a pound.

Hwang made an observation, "[Kim Jong-il] killed a man who was considered to be very progressive. Park pushed for an open market system. Kim instituted the new currency system to squash the rising tide of the market. His actions clearly demonstrate that he is not interested in people and what they have to go through to survive every day."

Hwang also observed that Kim Jong-il might be receiving reports that had been exaggerated or falsified ever since he suffered a stroke in 2008. There are rumors that Kim's recent interest in economic activities and agricultural production prompted his subordinates to concoct glowing pictures for him.

When he visited a poultry farm in October 2009, Party officials from Pyong Buk Province had the cooperative farm collect all the chickens from the area before he arrived with his entourage of cadres. Kim was very pleased with the robust poultry production and their plans for distributing the chicken meat to the public. In January 2010, he visited a flour factory in Pyongyang and stayed much longer than expected, putting the factory staff in a difficult spot. They ran out of grain supply, and they had to sneak the finished flour sacks back on the line and reprocess them in order to keep the factory running.

These episodes and others may have been an indication that Kim Jong-il was losing his grip on what was going on. What was intriguing and emblematic was that his heir apparent, Kim Jong-un, was said to be reviewing the reports on security and police matters before he sent them on to his father. "He doesn't want to burden his father with bad news" was the explanation. Kim Jong-il himself had used the same sort of reasoning for circumventing his father back when he was consolidating his own powerbase.

What goes around comes around, as the saying goes, and Kim Jong-il would have been furious when he realized that he was a lame-duck leader. Hwang told me, "Kim Il-sung went through the same process. After a while, Kim Il-sung began paying deference to Kim Jong-il. It was pitiful. I felt disgusted when I read the poem he wrote for his son's fiftieth birthday."

Ultimately, Kim Il-sung wanted to leave behind a one-of-a-kind socialist republic for his son. Kim Jong-il also wanted what every good father wants—to pass on his good name and legacy to the next generation.

So far, the Kims' most notable legacy is a personality cult that borders on the same kind of religious fervor seen during the Middle Ages. Whether the same zeal and passion will pass on to the next generation is questionable.

In terms of quality of life of the people, the first two Kims have failed miserably, and there is no indication that the third Kim would fare any better than his predecessors. The third time may not be the charm, in this case.

In its effort to legitimize the third Kim, the Party's propaganda machine is focusing on building and reinforcing the concept of the Super Kim bloodline. The trouble with being a superman, though, is that it is hard to live up to all the promises, like Kim Jong-il's recent campaign for "Rice and meat soup for everyone."

Eventually he must deliver the goods in order to retain his status as the messiah for the People's Republic. People are tired of the years of empty talk and empty stomachs. The truth of the matter is that there are not enough resources in North Korea for it to become "the world's strongest army" and to feed everyone rice and meat soup.

Hwang had this advice for Kim Jong-il: "It is time for Kim Jong-il to step aside and give people a chance. People were fooled once already. Three million people gave their lives. They will not be fooled again. Never mind the paradise on earth; people no longer have that illusion. They just want food. You cannot eat nuclear missiles."

That is not to say that a popular uprising is imminent. As things are today, only the lower-echelon military people have a chance to mount any sort of significant resistance against Kim Jong-un and the Party, according to Hwang. Other than the military, no other sector is capable of rising up against the current regime. The religious sector, intellectuals, and business sector are constantly under watch.

Old-timers and ex-partisans understand what is going on, and they do not like the impoverished condition the country is in. They are not excited about the prospect of a dynastic transition of power either.

Like Hwang, they have seen corruption of power up close. It is only natural in the twilight of their years that they reflect on what they have witnessed versus the republic they had set out to build way back when they were full of ideals and stood behind Kim Il-sung. Kim Jong-il was a disappointment for them, and no doubt some of them regretted having supported him simply because he was Kim Il-sung's son. They now know that Kim Jong-il was a mistake from the beginning and that they should not have put him in the position of power. He lacked the qualifications necessary to become a well-balanced proletarian dictator, after all. He has been mastering this ruling for thirty-five years, starting as an intern under his father's tutelage, and was intimately familiar with all the facets of running his country and the 23 million people in it. He truly knew it like the back of his hand, one might say.

That's exactly what the problem was. He was so familiar with his job that he treated everything like his personal property—his party, his army, his palaces, his cars, his people, his country, and so on. Consequently, his personal views and thoughts took precedence over the nation's constitution, laws, and rules. He established Kim-Il-sung-ism and Ten Principles in honor of his father, which in turn governed the daily lives of the masses from top to bottom. More than anything else, though, he demanded loyalty from his subjects, generously rewarding those who were loyal to him. Betray him, and he was unmerciful.

People naturally wanted to be on his good side, some out of fear for their lives and some out of genuine devotion. Those who have benefited from his generosity will praise him endlessly, and those who were tortured and jailed in political prisons will condemn him, silently at least. This was how he maintained his supremacy over his subjects.

Why did he do it?

Hwang said it was a habit. He has been the supreme ruler for so long that he could not imagine anything else. Nor could his cronies and the masses.

CHAPTER 10

LET MY PEOPLE GO!

D emocratization of North Korea is a movement Hwang created to prepare the people of North Korea in the event that the Kim Jong-il regime collapsed or the two Koreas became unified. Whatever the outcome, it needs to be understood that the North Korean people have been under Kim's spell for decades, and they badly need debriefing.

It would take a long time to reverse the course for North Korea, and Hwang felt that the process had to begin now. The North Korean people must be made cognizant of the fact that their elite leaders have deliberately isolated them as masses from the rest of world in order to maintain their control.

Hwang knew he was fighting an uphill battle, because transforming a nation of people was easier said than done. He recognized that it would take years to bring North Koreans out of their collective shell and have them join the rest of the modern world. As a result, Hwang tirelessly wrote and spoke about democratizing North Korea while he trained and mentored young defectors to become leaders in preparation for the day they would return to North Korea.

Kim Jong-il did not like what Hwang was doing, though, and had a standing order for his special forces to assassinate Hwang. Even though Hwang's effort had hardly made any difference in transforming North Korea, nevertheless Kim Jong-il regarded him dangerous enough to send assassins to kill him.

However, Hwang was not deterred. He was only concerned about setting North Koreans free from its failed dictatorship. Besides the assassins from Pyongyang, he had to deal with his opponents within South Korea, politicians and unification advocates who felt that he was interfering with the process of normalizing relations with the North.

Former president Kim Dae-jung had severely restricted Hwang's movements, citing "safety concerns for Hwang." But such concern was a disingenuous attempt to keep him under virtual house arrest. Hwang often lamented the "bad timing" of his defection, the year of a presidential election in which Kim Dae-jung (a person he had met many years before in Japan) became president. Kim Dae-jung, a proponent of appeasement policy, had no use for Hwang's point of view and forbade him from engaging in any activity of a political nature or even speaking to reporters, for fear of antagonizing Kim Jong-il. For Kim Dae-jung, staying on good terms with Kim Jong-il was more important than what Hwang had to offer. Kim Dae-jung would not have hesitated a minute to sacrifice Hwang if Kim Jong-il had asked Kim Dae-jung to return Hwang to North Korea.

Roh Moo-hyun, the president who followed Kim Dae-jung, was also a proponent of the sunshine policy in the name of peaceful unification. He too restricted Hwang's activities and closely monitored him. However, he did allow Hwang to visit the United States. The latest government led by Lee Myung-bak was more amenable to Hwang's initiative, and Hwang had felt much freer to pursue his mission. Hwang became more active, lecturing and broadcasting about events surrounding North Korea, ranging from nuclear tests to a treatise on collectivism.

Hwang asserted that the world was paying too much attention to Kim Jong-il when he exploded nuclear weapons or fired off missiles. "[Kim Jong-il] thrives on attention and becomes energized by it. We should ignore him." Hwang observed that Kim needed the international attention in order to bolster his "world-class" image among his masses. According to Hwang, Kim's "victories" in the international theater helped him overcome many problems on the domestic front, mainly the shortage of food and energy.

Hwang long thought that China held the key to what happened in North Korea and that the United States must work closely with China in order to resolve the North Korean issue. His words of advice to the United States: "Deal with China rather than Kim Jong-il because direct talks with Kim Jong-il will only result in strengthening him. If China severs its relations with Kim Jong-il, he would be finished within one year. However, China doesn't want to take over North Korea. It has its own 1.3 billion people to worry about, and North Korea is the last thing they want to absorb into the mix. The US and South Korea should get close to China in order to break up its alliance with North Korea. That is the way to get at Kim Jong-il. The US and China must lead the democratization effort in North Korea."

He advised that "A Free Trade Agreement between South Korea and China would have a tremendous impact on resolving the North Korean issues, although the experts claim that such agreement would bring about a loss of $100 million. Instead of looking at it as an economic loss, they should deem the $100 million as political investment.

"China and North Korea appear to be allies, but they are not joined at the hips in terms of ideology. China is out to protect its own national interest and does not want a war on the peninsula. Back when South Korea and China normalized their relations in 1992, a North Korean emissary went to China and pleaded with them to wait one year before normalizing relations with the South, but the Chinese government led by Jiang Zemin said no. Everyone in Pyongyang was shocked at the Chinese, who supposedly were their ideological ally. I understood the Chinese. You cannot eat ideology. They wanted a better life for their people … and investment and technology from South Korea."

Currently, China is the largest trading partner for South Korea, and the two countries are discussing a free trade agreement, which would bind the two even closer. They have come a long way together from the Korean War, once archenemies when China, then known as Red China, mounted a surprise counterattack against the advancing UN and the South Korean forces. The Chinese soldiers saved Kim Il-sung's army from certain defeat, and Mao Zedong lost a son in the process. Despite this bitter past, the two nations have found common grounds for cooperation, while North and South Korea, who share the common language and customs, continue to have problems.

Hwang often talked about the dichotomy that existed in the Korean peninsula, referring to the South as "heaven" and the North, "hell." Hwang would lament, "Kim Jong-il is such a fool. The Chinese tried to tell him, 'Come with us, come with us,' but he refuses to listen. He calls them Chinese dogs, betrayers of true socialism, they're worse than the dogs of the South."

Still, China continues to help Kim Jong-il. China joined the UN sanction against Kim following his nuclear tests. China tried to dissuade

Kim from carrying out the nuclear tests, but Kim went ahead with them anyway.

"China helps him just enough so his regime doesn't completely collapse," Hwang would say. In that sense, China wants the status quo, as do the South Korean supporters of the Kim Jong-il regime. To them, stability in North Korea is more important than anything else, and they want to prop up Kim Jong-il so they don't have to deal with the potential chaos located so close to their border.

As far as Hwang was concerned, what had begun as utopian paradise back in the days of Kim Il-sung was now facing certain collapse. There were plenty of reminders and object lessons regarding failed socialist dreams, the breakup of former Soviet Union and all its satellite nations that have abandoned their Marxist ideals. Whether North Korea would follow the Soviet model when it collapses, nobody knows. There probably won't be any talk about *perestroika* or *glasnost,* though. One thing for sure: the natural inclination for North Koreans is to fill the vacuum left by the strong central leadership with another dictatorship. It will take them many years to realize that they do not need to replace a dictatorship with another. The absence of the strong, centralized control will contribute to the confusion and chaos, and truths about the Kim dynasty will add to their disillusionment about its corrupt class system, and they will wonder if there was true equality, ever. At the same time, former elites will brood about their lost privileged life, best food, fancy homes, expensive cars, best schools for their children, while the rest of the country, poverty-stricken, struggles for new direction.

How would the North Korean people behave when the system goes under? Will they flee? Will they riot and loot? What about the gulags and 150,000 political prisoners? Will they be released? What about schools? Hospitals? Will buses and trains run? Most of all, what will they eat?

These questions and others need to be addressed, and plans must be formulated and ready for implementation in the event that North Korea ceases to function as a society altogether. Hwang was very confident that North Koreans would do fine. "Once the new system is in place, they will be fine. In ten years, they will be right up there with the South. They're Koreans, too, and we already know what Koreans are capable of, how strong their will to survive is. We have had the miracle of the Han River. We'll get the miracle of the Dae Dong River, too."

Hwang counted on their irrepressible will to survive, which they have shown time and again despite the harshest circumstances they continue to experience. He believed that North Korean people would react to the sixty years of centralized oppression with a tremendous bang—as in the "big bang theory"—and that new heroes and leaders would emerge during the process of decentralization in all sectors: agriculture, industry, medicine, education, communication, and transportation.

The decentralization process would also apply to politics. The Workers' Party will have to dissolve, and new democratic parties will be installed in its place, followed by popular election. This is also contingent on a full-scale campaign to help the people understand democratic principles so that they can properly participate in the electoral process.

Hwang's role in this regard would have been important because of his familiarity with both systems. He knew exactly what North Koreans needed; he did not have to guess or rely on hypothetical theories. Many scenarios and hypothetical situations with respect to new North Korea have been bantered about recently, but they do not directly address the needs of the people. Rather, these theories have dealt with abstract things like unitizing economy, the theory of "functionalism" in connection with the formulation of EEC, German-style unification, and unification via the sunshine policy, unification by forming a federation consisting of two distinct states, and so on.

Hwang did not give these hypothetical theories much chance for success, because they were based on political expediency rather than the needs of the people. Kim Dae-jung's sunshine policy, for instance, was supposed to persuade Kim Jong-il to reform his economic policies, but it didn't happen. We now know that Kim Jong-il never meant to abandon his planned economy all along, even as he discussed economic cooperation with Kim Dae-jung during their summit.

Kim Dae-jung was the man of the hour when he returned from Pyongyang following his summit with Kim Jong-il. In his report to the South Korean electorate, he said, "If we go into North Korea and build their railroad, solve their problems with electric power, roads, harbors, and communication systems, our economy will expand to the entire peninsula beyond our border, thereby producing huge benefits for both North and South."

Hence South Korea invested 1 billion dollars annually for ten years without any real progress in changing Kim Jong-il's mind about economic reform. It turned out to be an expensive lesson for South Korean taxpayers to learn that the sunshine policy was doomed from the start.

Hwang believed that the sunshine policy, like many unification schemes advanced by various experts and advocates, failed because it was inspired and carried out for political gain by both Kims. In the end, he believed that the North Korean people must be the ultimate beneficiary of any policy. Before anything, though, Hwang and other defectors have long felt that North Koreans first need to unlearn the Ten Principles of Kim Il-sung and substitute in its place the concept of democratic principles, i.e., the government *of* the people, *for* the people, and *by* the people. Someday …

Epilogue
In commemoration of
Hwang Jang-yop
By K.J. Sohn, chief editor of *DailyNK*

Hwang Jang-yop

October 10, 2010 will go down as a significant day in the history of the Korean Peninsula. Its significance is twofold: First, the date represents the sixty-fifth anniversary of the founding of the Workers' Party. The Party held a huge celebration in Pyongyang on this date by showcasing a grand military parade. It also announced to the world that the Kim dynasty would continue by making Kim Jong-un the official successor. Kim Jong-un, together with his father, Kim Jong-il, and his grandfather, Kim Il-sung, would complete what we call the devil's triangle.

Second, on this same day, Hwang Jang-yop, the leader of the Democratization of North Korea movement, passed away in Seoul. He had defected from North Korea on February 12, 1997, in order to prevent another war in the Korean Peninsula and to facilitate peaceful unification of the two Koreas. The news of his defection made headlines across Asia, and his detailed accounts of the oppression, gulags, false propaganda, and the widespread famine followed. He became the new light of hope for the 23 million North Korean people.

However, despite his tireless efforts for more than thirteen years, the movement for the democratization of North Korea did not blossom the way it should have. With the selection of Kim Jong-un as the successor to the Kim monarchy, one might even say that the movement has fallen backward. But is the movement finished? I don't believe so. The future for democratization looks bright, because Teacher Hwang planted many seeds in the name of human rights and democratization for the people of North Korea. Those seeds have sprouted and are growing. It won't be long before we see the fruits of his labor. His death will beget many new lives, and the movement will go on.

I met Teacher Hwang for the first time in April 1999. I was then a research fellow at the Unification Policy Center at the National Intelligence Service of Korea. After the initial meeting, we met regularly every week, four hours on Tuesdays and two on Thursdays, until 2004.

We discussed communist ideology, its ruling system, Kim Il-sung, Kim Jong-il, open-market system, human rights issues, democratization, nuclear weapons issues, peaceful unification of the two Koreas, and international cooperation in resolving these problems. As a former reporter for eleven years at *DongA Daily News*, I had become the chief editor of *DailyNK*, an Internet news website specializing in North Korean issues. We continued to meet regularly until he passed away in 2010. I had the honor of serving him as his research secretary for eleven years.

As his research secretary, I learned that he was a remarkable philosopher and humanist. He envisioned a free society for 23 million fellow countrymen and worked hard to replace the dictatorial monarch with a democratic form of government.

In 2003, when he visited Washington, DC, he endeavored to explain his strategy for democratizing North Korea to the US officials in the State Department, the Department of Defense, and to CIA personnel. He lamented afterward, "The American officials know too little about the situation in North Korea. He said that the American officials are only concerned about the nuclear weapons, and they think they can negotiate with Kim Jong-il." He added, "Americans do not understand clearly that the only way to resolve the nuclear problem is to replace the Kim dynasty with an open democratic governing system."

This nuclear problem began in the early 1990s and persisted for eighteen years. There have been numerous attempts to come up with a resolution, including the Geneva Agreement, the six-party talks, the 9.19 Communiqué, and the 10.3 Agreement. The end result was two nuclear weapon tests and Kim Jong-il achieving for North Korea the status as a "de-facto nuclear weapon state" at the same time the six-party talks were going on. The big question became how did this problem take a turn for the worse during the six-party talks?

My guess is that the US government officials didn't understand the fact that the nuclear weapons and the Kim dynasty are inseparable. Simply put, getting rid of the nuclear weapons is synonymous with getting rid of the Kim dynasty. Placement of a democratic system by the people of North Korea is the only way to solve the nuclear weapons problem. It is up to the international community, mainly South Korea, the United States, China, and Japan, to help the people install a new government. Teacher Hwang explained this concept to the Americans again in 2010. I have come to think that Hwang's solution to the nuclear problem will actually work on other problems as well, e.g., the famine, human rights violations, and improvement of life in general. Installation of a democratic government in North Korea would contribute toward economic prosperity in the region as well as ensure its stability.

I think Teacher Hwang's insights into the nature of the Kim Jong-il dictatorship will help everyone, and I summarize them here:

- Kim Jong-il made a prison out of the entire country by way of practicing rigid, monarchist dictatorship. Kim Jong-il regarded himself as a "dictatorial genius" and had tremendous confidence that he could do anything he desired. He had complete disregard for international laws and agreements. He believed that his wishes became law.

- Kim Jong-il believed that a dictator had special rights, even allowing him to conduct international criminal activities. Violating human rights, selling contraband, printing counterfeit currency, and abducting foreigners were within his rights. His termination of non-nuclear proliferation treaty in actuality was only a minor event for him.

- Some people in South Korea try to analyze the importance of race (Koreans, North and South) versus the importance of alliance (South Korea and the United States). This is a meaningless analysis. In an exercise like this, one should consider whether or not such analysis is based on democratic principles. Racial alliance that is not founded on democratic principles is meaningless.

- Resolving human rights problems should take priority over the nuclear problem. Sometimes, we avoided criticizing the human rights condition in the North because we didn't want to upset Kim Jong-il. This was wrong. Allowing Kim to violate human rights was just as bad as committing the crime ourselves.

- If North Korea opens up, the market economy will prosper, and the dictatorship will cease to exist.

- China holds the key to the life and death of the Kim monarchy. Without China's cooperation, it will be difficult to reform North Korea. If China and the United States work together, they can solve the nuclear problem. The United States must persuade China that the most important element is for China to get rid of the Kim dictatorship and adopt "the open policy."

Teacher Hwang Jang-yop, the Man I Knew

Hwang Jang-yop was born in Gang Dong near Pyongyang and studied at the Kim Il-sung University Philosophy Department and Moscow University. When he returned from Moscow, he became the first PhD in the history of Kim Il-sung University. He then became the dean of the Philosophy Department, followed by the presidency. He later became the secretariat of the Ideology Committee of the Party Central, international secretariat, and the president of the Presidium of the Supreme People's Committee.

He was a leading Party official, as well as philosopher. He pioneered "anthropocentric philosophy" and spread its essence in South Korea. His philosophy will be studied in many countries, as he delves into questions like "What is philosophy's role in humankind?" and "What is a human being?" in a way that nobody has done before.

He also had a good sense of humor. I recall a session in which we were discussing children's education. I asked him to say a few words for the young generation. I intended to pass on his words to my daughter. Teacher Hwang wrote, "Have a big dream, give your best effort, then you'll become a great person" on a piece of paper and gave it to me. I was thinking that it would be a good present for my daughter.

As it turned out, however, he wrote it for me. He gave his note to me, saying, "Mr. Sohn, always dream big." I told him, "But Teacher Hwang, I am already forty-two," implying that his words belonged to someone much younger than me. He replied, "I'm approaching eighty, so I am more inclined to contemplate about my death, but you still have many years to go. So you would benefit more by dreaming big." I took the paper from him, feeling like a middle-school child.

★★★

Holding seminars with young scholars was the single most important thing for him. There were four of us at a seminar in 2001, three philosopher types (Sunoo Hyun, Kim Won-sik, and Lee Shin-chul) and me. Teacher Hwang habitually told us that "Man must be careful not to waste his time without a goal in his life."

Whenever he said this, he always added, "One must not waste his valuable time by drinking and smoking." He never touched a drop of alcohol or puffed a cigarette in his life. Whenever he said this, all four of us remained very quiet. At that time, with the exception of Dr. Sunoo Hyun, we drank and were heavy smokers. Teacher Hwang didn't know this about us.

One day after his usual admonishment against drinking and smoking, he asked me out of the blue, "Ah, Mr. Sohn, do you drink liquor?"

I knew that he detested drinking and smoking, but I had no choice but to tell him the truth. I said, "Yes, I drink often."

Then he asked, "Do you smoke cigarettes?"

"Yes, of course."

He didn't look too happy. He turned to Dr. Lee next. He asked, "Do you drink and smoke too?"

Dr. Lee drank more than I did. He replied, "Yes, I drink a lot and very often."

Teacher Hwang remained quiet for a while. He finally turned to Dr. Kim and asked him, as if he was the last hope, "How about you?"

Dr. Kim waited a little and said, "I drink like a fish."

Teacher Hwang was puzzled a bit about Dr. Kim's reference to fish. He turned to me for an explanation, and I said, "Dr. Kim drinks the most here. He is the best drinker."

Following that day, Teacher Hwang stopped saying, "One must not waste his valuable time by drinking and smoking." Instead, he began saying, "One must not waste his valuable time by doing drugs and things."

Of course none of us did drugs. He didn't admonish us directly for our drinking and smoking habits. That was his roundabout way of telling us he still didn't approve of our drinking and smoking.

I would like to share another story about Teacher Hwang. One autumn day in 1999, a cable TV station requested Teacher Hwang to appear for a talk show regarding North Korean issues. He was not used to appearing in front of a TV camera, so he asked me for my opinion. "Mr. Sohn, what do you think about the cable station?"

He rarely appeared on television, and I thought that if he were to appear on television, he should go on major stations like KBS that command a large audience. So I told him, "It'd be better to wait for a major station." I also added that his counterpart in the talk show should be at least a college president or someone like that, considering the fact that he was the former president of Kim Il-sung University.

Teacher Hwang wasn't excited about going on the show either. He had a completely different reason than mine, though. He said, "The man who is supposed to be my counterpart … he's too old."

I was curious about his counterpart's age. "How old is he?"

"He is seventy-eight."

"Pardon me?" I replied with a question, as Teacher Hwang himself was seventy-seven, just one year younger.

Teacher Hwang added, "He's just too old." Teacher Hwang saw himself as a young man to the end.

★★★

Teacher Hwang was Kim Il-sung's secretary during the 1950s and 1960s. In this role, he often accompanied Kim to China. He frequently conversed with Mao, Cho Enlai, and Deng Hsiao Peng. Deng was the secretary for Mao.

On a visit with Mao during the 1960s, Mao was bragging to Kim Il-sung, "Soon, China is going to overtake Britain in productiveness," and talked excitedly about the merits of the communist way of doing things.

That day, Mao's main topic was about a new, perfect way of solving the food problem in a short period of time. He explained about a new method of planting rice, by digging deeper and burying two plants on top of each other. He said the rice production would double in the same amount of space. He went on and on, "China can make the ideal communist society for sure."

The meeting dragged on, and before anyone realized, it was well past lunchtime, and the participants became hungry. Proper etiquette in the East calls for serving the meal before the guests become hungry. Realizing that it was well past the mealtime, Deng went to Mao and whispered that it was lunchtime.

Mao nodded and excitedly repeated his story to Kim Il-sung and how wonderful his new system was. After thirty minutes, Deng approached Mao and whispered again that it was time to eat lunch. Mao nodded again and went right back to his story. Thirty or forty minutes later, Deng went to Mao the third time and said, "We have to eat now."

Then Mao became angry and shouted, "Comrade Deng! Eat, eat, eat. That's all you think about!" Deng was startled. He quietly left the room.

Teacher Hwang recalled this drama and said, "Mao, at that moment, was in a state of fantasy created by his own thoughts. In the end, Mao's planting idea failed miserably. Many people died of starvation. It's ironic that Deng is the one who transformed China's economy."

★★★

Teacher Hwang worked very hard these last thirteen years, inspiring many young people about the democratization of North Korea. He left behind an impressive list of books, and his treatise on anthropocentric philosophy is an important topic of discussion in the field of philosophy.

He was the source of inspiration for Han Ki-hong, Kim Young-hwan, Hong Jin-pyo, and me to create the *DailyNK,* the first Internet news organization specializing in North Korea.

Over twenty thousand North Korean expatriates considered Teacher Hwang their leader in democratizing North Korea. I give my humble bow to the man who built a solid foundation for the future generation to finish his work. May Teacher Hwang rest in peace.

AFTERWORD

December 18, 2011, 7:03 PM

I was in my study translating a Korean short story, when my son in the next room yelled out "Kim Jong-il is dead!"

I thought he was playing pranks again, which he is known to do now and then, and I replied with a grunt, "Sure, tell me another one." I had submitted the manuscript of this book to my publisher two weeks before, and the editors were in the process of reviewing the manuscript, which made it a tense period of time for me. My son was trying to reduce my tenseness, I thought, and I appreciated his gesture.

"News flash, dad. It just came on the internet." I could tell he was not kidding. I stopped what I was doing and switched to news bulletin, and sure enough, North Korean central news agency made an announcement about Kim's death.

I couldn't believe it. I was certain that he would live at least for another ten years following his recovery from his stroke in 2008, judging by his long train trips to China and to Russia. I had marveled at his excellent medical team, how resourceful they were. I was shocked to learn about his death. Immediately, questions flooded in from my friends: Did you hear about Kim's death? What do you think? What's going to happen to North Korea now?

I told them that I was shocked at his sudden death because he had appeared so healthy these recent months. I told them that there were questionable things about his death, such as the exact time and date, location of his death. Was he really on his way to or coming back from a working trip? Did he really die on his train at 8:30 in the morning like they said? Didn't a satellite photo show that his train had not moved at all? Why did they wait three days to announce his death? What were the party leaders talking about during those three days?

Many questions came and went.

The story was a headliner for CNN, MSNBC, Fox News, but none of them addressed my questions. They were more interested in things like who was going to take over now that Kim Jong-il was dead. They talked about young Kim Jong-un who was in line to succeed power. Jong-un was the youngest of the three sons, but his father picked him to rule the country, they said. They showed Jong-un at the head of reception line receiving endless guests who came to pay respect to Kim Jong-il and mourn for the dead.

According to Korean customs, the oldest son should be at the head of the reception line, I was thinking. Where were his older brothers, Jong-nam and Jong-chol? Their names didn't appear on the list of 232 members that formed the funeral committee, either.

More questions.

I called K.J. Sohn, my coauthor in Seoul, but he didn't answer. When he finally called back he said he had been in meetings all day.

I asked him, "Anything new from your contacts in the North?"

"It's difficult to get through. Cell phones are either dead or they're hiding them because the police is tracking them down. Jong-un issued an order to seal off the border. He declared a state of emergency and ordered to shoot anyone who tries to cross the river without authorization. He also shut down all the markets."

"Tough guy act, I see."

"He is making his presence known."

"He is not trying to win popularity, I suppose."

"Well, it looks like he is using this mourning period as his platform to consolidate his power. Party cadres are lining up to pledge their loyalty to him."

"I read an article by one of your reporters that people cry in front of Kim Jong-il's shrine, but smile when they go home."

"Yes, I read that, too. Our contact says, when Kim Il-sung died in 1994, two out of three people cried for him. This time, just one of three."

"So, if Jong-un tries to continue his father's policies, he is in for a rough time."

"Well, he is stuck with his father's policies, and his grandfather's before that. Because he inherited his 'Leader' status from his grandfather through his father, and he has to prove that he is a supreme leader. In the eyes of the people, his father Kim Jong-il was not a great leader that his grandfather was. Kim Il-sung cared about people, like Mr. Hwang said. Mass starvation was inconceivable under Kim Il-sung's leadership. Three million people starved to death during the Kim Jong-il era, but he managed to 'pass' as a great leader by way of false propaganda and violent means."

"So, how can Jong-un prove himself as a leader?"

"I think he has run out of options."

"What do you mean?"

"Look at what he is inheriting. A broken-down system that is ready to collapse with the exception of the Pyongyang district and its 3 million plus population. Thanks to his father, he's already lost the rest of the country. After the famine, people in the countryside have sustained themselves by creating their own marketplace and they don't need the central leadership, the benevolent father Kim Il-sung, or Kim Jong-il. The people have been fending for themselves and they are not going to put their trust in the party again. The party's propaganda machine is busy promoting 'Comrade Jong-un in the like image of his father the great general,' but I seriously doubt if people would follow Jong-un to the end. The privileged set in Pyongyang would follow him for the time being, as long as they feel it is beneficial for them to do so. There is no ideology or purpose that binds the people and Jong-un together."

"You don't think he is going to make it, do you?"

"Not as a SuRyong. The SuRyong system, the proletarian dictatorship, is over now."

"But Jong-un has to go that way because he has no other choice. He is the inheritor of great leadership."

"Correct."

"He is stuck in that role."

"Yes."

"How does he perform this role at his age?"

"It will be difficult. His father most likely put all the mechanisms in place for Jong-un to follow, but will the men Kim Jong-il handpicked follow Jong-un with same kind of loyalty?"

"Good point. When Kim Il-sung died, Kim Jong-il immediately displaced his father's staff with his own. Jong-un didn't get to do that."

"Because he hasn't had a chance to develop his own team of people."

"He is too young. How about his aunt Kim Kyoung-hui, his uncle Jang Song-thaek, Kim Yong-choon, and Ri Yong-ho, etc.?"

"He needs their support to make it. I think, right now, he needs them more than they need him. He can't exercise his authority like his father had. He can't send Jang to a re-indoctrination camp like his father had, for instance."

"No, he is not his father. He won't be able to exert the same kind of authority. Basically, he has to deal with his father's infrastructure whether he likes it or not."

"Unless..."

"Unless?"

"Unless he wipes out everyone."

"Everyone?"

"For instance, he could purge anyone who might lean toward a Chinese-style market system. That would provide him a good basis for a wholesale purge."

"I can imagine Kim Jong-il warning Jong-un not to trust the Chinese."

"Kim Jong-il said that the Chinese infiltration is one hundred times worse than the American imperialist spies. I'd imagine that Kim Jong-il stressed that point to his son over and over."

"Yes, and the Russians. He didn't trust the Russians, either."

"As evidenced by his purging of pro-Russian generals and officers."

"Does Jong-un have the balls to carry out purges like that?"

"We'll have to wait and see. But, if he wants absolute control, he'd have to seal off the borders, wipe everyone out, abolish the markets that have sprung up all over the country, cut off all the commercial trading across the border, and reestablish central planning."

"That would mean a lot of killings."

"Yes."

"Or else, he will have to buy into the marketeering that is going on, establish himself in the marketplace and come up with his own plans for a market system that people would follow."

"That's the other option for him. But what are the chances of that happening? Even if he came up with his own plans for reforming economy, people will not follow him."

"So, either way, he will have rough time establishing his leadership. I see what you mean by his running out of options."

"Like I said, SuRyong-style totalitarianism is dead. I think it's just a matter of time before Jong-un finds himself alone without anyone for him to lead."

We went on like this for a while longer, hypothesizing and rambling on about the new political landscape of North Korea sans Kim Jong-il. We lamented that Mr. Hwang wasn't here to give us his insights about what was going to happen to North Korea.

He would have said, "We have to focus on what's good for the people. People come first." He had repeatedly told us that dynastic succession of power was a ludicrous concept, often referring to Jong-un as "that young kid." He would have watched on television all the hoopla about Jong-un and exhorted, "Outrage! Where is all the outrage?"

I miss Mr. Hwang.

APPENDICES

I. Who's Who in Kim Family's Circle of Power

II. Writings by Hwang Jang-Yop

III. *Aphorisms of the Great Leader Comrade Kim Jong-il*

APPENDIX I:

WHO'S WHO IN KIM FAMILY'S CIRCLE OF POWER

Kim Kyoung-hui

Born 1946, she is Kim Jong-il's sister; member of the Political Bureau and department director of the Workers' Party Central Committee. She oversees the Light Manufacturing Department of the Party Central. She recently received the rank of four-star general, together with Kim Jong-un and Choe Ryong-hae.

Jang Song-thaek

Born 1946, he is the right arm of Kim Jong-il, also the husband of Kim Kyoung-hui, Kim Jong-il's sister. He has Kim Jong-il's complete trust and is one of the most powerful members in the Workers' Party. An alternate member of the Political Bureau and vice chairman of the DPRK National Defence Commission, he is very influential in matters of personnel and the Party organization. He is an accomplished accordionist and is interested in art. His oldest brother, Jang Song-woo, is the commander of the Third Army responsible for defending the Pyongyang area. His second older brother, Jang Song-gil, is the political officer for the Tenth Army.

Ri Yong-ho

Member of the Presidium of the Political Bureau of the Central Committee of the Workers' Party, vice marshal of the Korean People's Army.

Kim Jong-gak

Born 1946, he is first vice director of the General Political Department of the People's Army, member of the Party Central Committee, vice director of the Department of Defence, member of the Supreme People's Assembly, full general of the People's Armed Forces, and a member of the Defence Commission.

Kim Young-choon

Born 1932, he is the minister of Defence Department, a member of the National Defence Commission, member of the Central Committee of the Party, vice marshal of the People's Armed Forces, and member of the Supreme People's Assembly. He graduated from ManGyungDae Revolutionary Academy and Kim Il-sung University. He became a member of the Central Committee of the Party in 1986, full general of the People's Army in 1992, chief of the Munitions Department in 1993, commander of the Sixth Army in 1994, and was promoted to minister of defence in 1995. Former hunting partner of Kim Jong-il, he is known to be impatient and strong-willed.

Ri Myoung-su

He is the minister of people's security of the DPRK National Defence Commission, general in the People's Army.

Together with Kim Young-choon, he ranks in the top two or three in the military hierarchy. He received instructions directly from Kim Jong-il without going through the General Political Bureau or the chief of the general staff. He accompanied Kim Jong-il on all the visits to military facilities.

Hyun Chol-hae

Born 1934, he is a full general, member of the Supreme People's Assembly, and Assembly Qualification Committee.

He graduated from ManGyungDae Revolutionary Academy and studied in Romania. He served in the security force for the Supreme

Command Center during the Korean War. He became the vice director of the Political Bureau of the Defence Department in 1965; director of Reserve Officers School in 1976; was appointed to commander of the People's Army Reserve in 1991 as a lieutenant general; was promoted to full general in 1995; and was appointed in 1996 to his current position of vice director of the Organization Guidance Department of the Political Bureau of the People's Army. He is known to be quiet and very loyal to Kim Jong-il.

Choe Ik-gyu

Born 1934, he is the vice director of the Information Department of the Central Committee of the Party. He also serves as the vice chairman of the Central Party Committee's Arts Council. He graduated from Pyongyang Teacher's College (Kim Hyung-jik Teacher's College), majoring in Russian literature. He was the director for Joseon Art Films from 1954 to 1956 and manager of film production for the Party's Information Department from 1957 to 1969 and was designated People's Hero in 1972. He was sacked for the escape of the kidnapped South Korean actress Choi Eun-hee and her husband and film director, Sheen Sang-ok. Kim Jong-il finally reinstated him to the Information Department in 1999.

Ju Kyu-chang

Born 1933, he is first vice director of the Defence Industry of the Party Central, member of the Defence Commission, and member of the Supreme People's Assembly.

Gang Sang-choon

Born 1940, he was the chief secretary for Kim Jong-il and vice director of the Organizational Guidance Department of the Central Party Committee. He managed all the personal items for Kim Jong-il and reviewed documents for Kim Jong-il as well as coordinating security matters. He has been Kim's shadow for twenty years.

Gang Ju-il (Gang Gwan-ju)

Born 1930, he is the Central Party Committee's director of external communications, vice chair for the Fatherland Peaceful Unification Committee, and member of the Supreme People's Assembly.

He graduated from Kim Il-sung University, majoring in history. He was appointed in 1975 as the manager of external communications of culture and first vice director of the Party External Communications Department in 1989. He has a strong personality and holds a positive view on North-South relations. He manages the funds sent to Kim Jong-il from the pro-North Korea activist organization (Jo Chung Ryeon) in Japan.

Kim Young-nam

Born 1928, he is a member of the Central Committee of the Party, member of the Political Bureau, member of the Supreme People's Assembly, and president of the Presidium of the Supreme People's Assembly.

He graduated from Kim Il-sung University and studied at Moscow University and Rostov University. He began at the International Department for the Central Committee of the Party in 1956 as the head secretary. He also worked at the Ministry of Foreign Affairs in 1962. In 1972, he became the director of the Party's International Department, and in 1978, he became a member of the Party Political Bureau. In 1982, he was appointed vice prime minister as well as the minister of foreign affairs. He led the North Korean delegation to the United Nations in 1991. He is known to possess an excellent memory and meticulous personality.

Kim Ki-nam

Born 1926, he is the secretary of the Party Central Committee, in charge of revolutionary history, and a member of the Supreme People's Assembly.

He graduated from ManGyungDae Revolutionary Academy and Kim Il-sung University, and studied at the Moscow International University. He began his career at the Ministry of Foreign Affairs in 1952 and moved on to be chief protocol officer in 1957. He was deputy director of the Science Education Department in 1961; editor-in-chief of *The Laborer* magazine in 1974; editor-in-chief for *Rodong Newspaper* in 1976; and became a member of the Central Committee of the Party in 1980. In 1992, he was the secretariat for the Party Information Department. He is known to be very conservative. He wrote and edited all speeches and correspondences for Kim Jong-il.

Gang Seok-ju

Born 1939, he is member of the Central Party Committee; first secretary of the Foreign Affairs Bureau, and member of the Supreme People's Assembly.

He majored in International Relations and English and studied in China. He became deputy director of foreign affairs in 1984, and became first secretary in 1986. In 1990, he led the North Korean delegation to the forty-fifth UN General Convention in Geneva; led the US–North Korea conference in 1993; participated in the Carter–Kim Il-sung meeting in 1994; and led the US–North Korea Nuclear Treaty in 1994. Relatively open-minded, he had to undergo a month-long indoctrination around 1992 or 1993. Ultimately, he recovered Kim Jong-il's trust and is a member of Kim Jong-il's secret party. He is the younger brother of Gang Seok-soong, director of the Party Historical Research Center.

Park Jae-kyung

Born 1933, he is the deputy general of the People's Army Political Bureau, Information Department. He graduated from Kim Il-sung University. He began as a political counselor in the Information Division in the Defence Department and became the chief information officer in 1980. He was promoted to brigadier general in 1985; was installed in the army political committee in 1989; was appointed to his current position in 1994; and became a full general in 1997. Devoted to Kim Jong-il, he released the poetic musical dance production called *Following the General to the End of the Road*. He is quiet and enjoys reading.

Kim Myung-guk

Born 1940, he graduated from the Kim Il-sung University and a military academy in Russia. He is member of the Defence Commission of the Party Central, member of the Supreme People's Assembly, and is considered a future candidate for joint chief of staff.

Jang Song-woo

Born 1935, he is vice marshal of the People's Army, member of the Central Committee of the Party, commander of the Third Army, and member of the Supreme People's Assembly. He graduated from ManGyungDae Revolutionary Academy and Kim Il-sung University. He served as the inspector general of the Defence Department in 1988;

chief of the Political Bureau of the Police Department in 1989; and became the commanding general of the Third Army. He served in the Korean War as a second lieutenant in the People's Second Army. Very military-minded, he is considered a major force in the military hierarchy. He is Jang Song-thaek's brother.

Jon ByongHo

Born 1926, he is the secretary of military industry of the Central Committee of the Party, member of the Central Committee of the Party, and member of National Defence Commission.

He graduated from ManGyungDae Revolutionary Academy and Kim Il-sung University and studied at Moscow University. He began his career in the WPK (Korean Workers' Party) Organizational Guidance Department in 1960 and rose to vice director of the department in 1968. He became a member of the Central Committee of the Party in 1980 and member of the Defence Commission in 1990.

A specialist in nuclear technology, military industry, and machinery, he has been managing the military industry for over twenty years. He is the brains behind the nuclear weapons development. He accompanied Kim Jong-il on a visit to China in 1983 and is one of the few civilians who sit in the meetings for the Military Commission of the Party Central.

Appendix II:
Writings by Hwang Jang-yop

1. Hwang Jang-yop, *Historical View of Society,* Korean, Sa Hoi Yeok Sa Gwan (Seoul: Shidae Jongshin, 2010).

2. Hwang Jang-yop and Lee Shin-chul, *Study of Logic,* Korean, Nohn Li Hak, (Seoul: Shidae Jongshin, 2010).

3. Hwang Jang-yop, *My View on Life,* Korean, In Saeng Gwan, (Seoul: Shidae Jongshin, 2010).

4. Hwang Jang-yop, *Hwang Jang-yop Memoirs,* Korean, Hwang Jang-yop Hoi Goh Rok, (Seoul: Shidae Jongshin, 2010).

5. Hwang Jang-yop, *My View of the World,* Korean, Seh Gye Gwan, (Seoul: Shidae Jongshin, 2010).

6. *Dialectical Materialism and Dialectical Art of War,* Korean, Byeon Jeung Bop-gwa Byeon Jeung Bop-jeok Jeon Ryank Jeon Sool, (Seoul: Shidae Jongshin, 2009).

7. Hwang Jang-yop, *Democracy and Communism,* Korean, English, Min Ju Ju Ui-wa Gong San Ju Eui, (Seoul: Shidae Jongshin, 2009).

8. Hwang Jang-yop, *Indictment of Kim Jong-il: Facts about Korean Peninsula in Hwang Jang-yop's Words,* Japanese, (Tokyo: Sankei Newspaper Publication, *2008).*

9. Hwang Jang-yop, *Democratization of North Korea and Democratic Strategy,* Korean, (Seoul: Shidae Jongshin, 2008).

10. Hwang Jang-yop, *Principles of Anthropocentric Philosophy,* Korean, In Gahn Joong Shim Cheol Hak Wol Lon, (Seoul: Shidae Jongshin, 2008).

11. Hwang Jang-yop, *Story of Philosophy for the Young,* Korean, Cheong Nyundeul-ul Wihan Cheol Hak Iyagi, (Seoul: Shidae Jongshin, 2007).

12. Hwang Jang-yop, *Dialectical Art of War,* Korean, Byeon Jeung Beop-jeok Jeon Lyak Jeon Sool Lon, (Seoul: Shidae Jongshin, 2006).

13. Hwang Jang-yop, *Truth and Lies about North Korea,* Korean, Buk Han-ui Gin Shil-gwa Heo Wi, (Seoul: Shidae Jongshin, 2006).

14. Hwang Jang-yop, *I Witnessed the True History: Hwang Jang-yop Memoir,* Korean, Hwang Jang-yop Hoi Go Rok/Na-neun Yeok Sa-ui Jin Li-reul Bo Ahtta. (Seoul: Shidae Jongshin, 2006).

15. Hwang Jang-yop, *Political Philosophy of Democracy,* Korean, Min Ju Ju Ui Jeong Chi Cheol Hak,(Seoul: Shidae Jongshin, 2005).

16. Hwang Jang-yop, *Historical View of Society,* Korean, Sa Hoi Yeok Sa Gwan,(Seoul: Shidae Jongshin, 2003).

17. Hwang Jang-yop, *Some Issues Regarding Anthropocentric Philosophy*, Korean, In Gahn Joong Shim Cheol Hak-ui Myeot Gaji Moon Je,(Seoul: Shidae Jongshin, 2003).

18. Hwang Jang-yop, *Hwang Jang-yop Strategy: How to Beat Kim Jong-il without a War,* Korean, Hwang Jang-yop-ui Dae Jeon Lyak: Kim Jong-il-gwa Jeon Jang Haji Ahn-ko Iki-seun Bahng Beop, (Seoul: Chosun Monthly 2003).

19. Hwang Jang-yop, *My View of the World,* Korean, Seh Gye Gwan,(Seoul: Shidae Jongshin, 2003).

20. Hwang Jang-yop, *Collapse of North Korea,* Japanese, (Tokyo: Kawade Shobo Shinsha Publishers inc., 2003).

21. Hwang Jang-yop, *My View on Life,* Korean, In Saeng Gwan, (Seoul: Shidae Jongshin, 2003).

22. Hwang Jang-yop, et al., *Is the TaeGeuk Flag Still Flying? Unification Plan of the 6.15 Summit Will Lead to a Certain War,* Korean, Ajigdo Tae Geuk Kineun Hwi Nal Ligo It neunga? 6.15 Seon Ondaero Tong Il Ha Get Damyeon Bahndeushi Nae Jeon-i Ironanda, (Seoul: Chosun Monthly, 2002).

23. Hwang Jang-yop, *Global Democratization and the Final War of the Mankind: Strategies for Global Democratization,* Korean, Seh Gye Min Ju Hwa-wa In Ryu-ui Majimahg Jeon Jang: Hwang Jang-yop-ui Seh Gye Min Ju Hwa Jeon Lyak, (Seoul: Shidae Jongshin, 2002).

24. Hwang Jang-yop, *Kim Jong-il's Declaration of War: Hwang Jang-yop's Memoir Series,* Japanese, (Tokyo: Bungeishunju, 2001).

25. Hwang Jang-yop, *Sunshine Siding with Darkness Cannot Illuminate: Hwang Jang-yop's Exposure of Secrets,* Korean, Hwang Jang-yop Birok Gong Gae: Uh Doom-ui Pyeon-i-doen Hatbyeot-un Uh Doom-eul Balkil-su-uhp-dah,(Seoul: Chosun Monthly, 2001).

26. Hwang Jang-yop, *The Life of the Korean People—More Valuable Than an Individual's: Peace and Unification*, Korean, *Gae In-ui Sang Myung boda Gwi Joong-han Minjok-ui Saeng Myung: Joguk Pyeong Hwa-wa Minjok Tong Il*, (Seoul: Shidae Jongshin, 1999)

27. Hwang Jang-yop, *I Witnessed the True History: Hwang Jang-yop Memoir*, Korean, Hwang Jang-yop Hoi Go Rok / Na-neun Yeok Sa-ui Jin Li-reul Bo Ahtta, (Seoul: HanWool, 1999)

28. Hwang Jang-yop, *Truth and Lies about North Korea*, Korean, Buk Han-ui Jin Shil-gwa Heo Wi (Seoul: Unification Policy Research Institute, 1998).

Appendix III:

Aphorisms of the Great Leader Comrade Kim Jong-il

(Quoted from [North] Korean-English Dictionary, Pyongyang, DPRK, with some editing for clarity in English usage)

1. Kim Jong-il's views on Su Ryong:

"Hoping for victory in a revolution without a leader is just like trying to grow flowers without the sun."

"No man is valuable without filial devotion, and no man is great without loyalty."

"Loyalty and filial devotion are the supreme qualities of a revolutionary."

"Single-hearted loyalty and filial devotion make the strongest weapon."

"The strongest loyalty and filial devotion produce the greatest happiness."

"A flaw can exist in a diamond, but never in one's loyalty and filial devotion."

"Heart, not money, will win loyalty."

"Disloyalty and undutifulness will bring death."

"Loyalty and filial devotion invigorate the revolution, whereas treasonous designs poison it."

"A loyal man comes to the fore in times of hardship."

"Loyalty will assert itself in a difficult situation, not during a time of peace.

"We are surrounded by loyalists and traitors alike."

"A loyal man lives forever, but a traitor lives short."

"A loyal man opens his heart; a traitor keeps his tightly closed."

"The loyal man speaks from his heart, while a traitor's heart is on the tip of his tongue."

"A treacherous man has a honeyed tongue but carries a knife in his belly."

"A loyal man and a traitor cannot live under the same roof nor eat from the same spot."

2. Political philosophy

"The JuChe idea is my political philosophy."

"Political philosophy is the compass of leadership."

"Poor-quality philosophy breeds poor-quality politics."

"Intelligence is what makes a great man a great beacon."

3. His point of view and on the masses

"Man, not money, is most valuable in the world."

"The masses are teachers of everything."

"Reality is a fine school, and the masses are the teachers."

"A miracle is not a gift from heaven; it is something inevitable wrought by the people."

"Work is done by the people; revolution is carried out by the masses."

"The eyes of the masses are always full of wisdom."

"Talent lies among the masses."

"After all, individual trees make a thick forest."

"The man who believes in the people gets to drink the elixir of life, while the man who turns his back on them will receive poison."

4. Role of ideology

"A great idea moves the world, not money or an atomic bomb."

"People's thoughts, not their social origin, carry out a revolution."

"The beauty of man lies in his ideas, not in his looks."

"Meaningful, noble ideas build noble character."

"Live not merely for today but for tomorrow."

"Nothing is impossible for a man who loves the future."

5. Self-determination and creativity

"Without independence of mind, one can create nothing new."

"A strong man trusts himself; a weak man relies on others."

"Live our own way; fight our own way; create our own way."

"A fool expects favors from others."

"Those who rely on themselves will prosper; those who rely on others will perish."

"A piece of iron in one's own house is better than a lump of gold in another's."

"Self-knowledge makes one a revolutionary; ignorance of self makes one a slave."

"He who knows himself grows strong, while he who is ignorant of himself becomes weak."

"The only way to measure the value of something new is to use a new yardstick."

"Empty words without creativity are like a thunder without rain."

"Do not wait for others to create something; present them with your own creations."

"Creation is discovery; imitation is repetition."

"The greatest human joy is in creation."

"A flaw in a creation remains an eternal blot on the creator's life."

"Do not regret after creating something; instead think twice before you create it."

6. Patriotism and JuChe

"Loving and treasuring our own things means patriotism and JuChe."

"A house with leaning pillars will fall down."

"Before becoming a scientist, first become an ardent patriot."

"Genuine patriotism is in the struggle for national reunification."

"Korea is an organism that can survive when whole, but cannot when divided."

7. Trust and love

"Trust produces loyalty; mistrust produces betrayal."

"Power and trust joined together will prevail over the heavens."

"Trust nurtures people."

"A man with no love for people can never carry out the revolution."

"Repaying love with love is a human virtue."

"The best medicine is the devotion of a doctor."

"There is an old saying that eight hundred *ryang* of gold will buy a house and one thousand *ryang* a neighbor, but one thousand *ryang* cannot buy a revolutionary comrade."

173

8. Conscience

"Conscience and heart are one and the same."

"Conscience mirrors behavior and tells truth from falsehood."

"Conscience is the gauge that measures what one is worth and how much confidence one can earn from others."

9. Knowledge and its role

"A man sees, hears, feels, and absorbs as much as he understands."

"A man can express only as much as he knows."

"Writing is a product of knowledge and passion."

"He who does not see the beauty of flowers will not learn to grow them."

10. Words and action

"What a man says shows what he is."

To speak is to act."

11. Passion, thought, and judgment

"Passion is the source of great creation."

"Think one hundred times and choose once."

"Weak judgment means strong prejudice."

"Dim eyes miss the target."

"Find a great thing in the commonplace; see a great thing in the small."

12. Education

"One does not automatically become a revolutionary just because one's parents are revolutionaries."

"Slowing down one step in the education of the younger generation means a ten-step delay in advancing the country."

13. Literary arts

"Literature is the art of language."

"A revolutionary poem can replace millions of spears and swords."

"True poetic words are found in the people's speech."

"The text of a song must be a refined poem."

"Stereotyping is a barrier between literature and the reader."

"The masses are the best critics."

"Art is a product of ideas and passion."

"Life goes hand in hand with music and song."

"Life without music is a garden without flowers."

"Music is the art of melody."

"Architecture is a composite art."

Made in the USA
Middletown, DE
04 January 2015